BROADWAY SONGS

**MELODY LINE, CHORDS AND LYRICS
FOR KEYBOARD • GUITAR • VOCAL**

HAL•LEONARD®

ISBN 0-634-01753-5

For all works contained herein:
Unauthorized copying, arranging, adapting, recording or public
performance is an infringement of copyright.
Infringers are liable under the law.

7777 W. BLUEMOUND RD. P.O. BOX 13819 MILWAUKEE, WI 53213

Visit Hal Leonard Online at
www.halleonard.com

Welcome to the PAPERBACK SONGS SERIES.

Do you play piano, guitar, electronic keyboard, sing or play any instrument for that matter? If so, this handy "pocket tune" book is for you.

The concise, one-line music notation consists of:

MELODY, LYRICS & CHORD SYMBOLS

Whether strumming the chords on guitar, "faking" an arrangement on piano/keyboard or singing the lyrics, these fake book style arrangements can be enjoyed at any experience level — hobbyist to professional.

The musical skills necessary to successfully use this book are minimal. If you play guitar and need some help with chords, a basic chord chart is included at the back of the book.

While playing and singing is the first thing that comes to mind when using this book, it can also serve as a compact, comprehensive reference guide.

However you choose to use this PAPERBACK SONGS SERIES book, by all means have fun!

CONTENTS

(contents continued)

(contents continued)

ALMOST PARADISE
from the Broadway Musical FOOTLOOSE

Words by DEAN PITCHFORD
Music by ERIC CARMEN

all my life___ I on - ly need - ed you?___
now we hold___ the fu - ture in ___ our hands.___

Oh, ___ al-most par - a - dise. ___ We're knock-ing on ___

heav-en's door. ___ Al-most par - a - dise. ___ How

could we ask ___ for ___ more? I

swear that I ___ can see ___ for - ev-er in your ___ eyes.

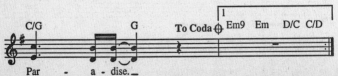

Par - a - dise. ___

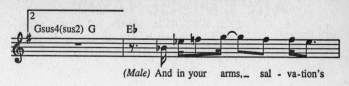

(Male) And in your arms,_ sal - va-tion's

not so far a - way._____

It's get - ting clos - er,

D.S. al Coda

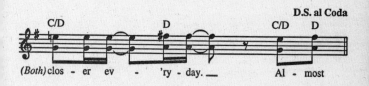

(Both) clos - er ev - 'ry - day._ Al - most

CODA

par - a - dise._

par - a - dise._

AIN'T MISBEHAVIN'

from AIN'T MISBEHAVIN'

Words by ANDY RAZAF
Music by THOMAS "FATS" WALLER and HARRY BROOKS

I'm sav-in' my love for you. _____

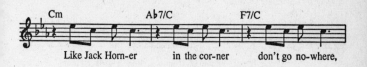

Like Jack Horn-er in the cor-ner don't go no-where,

what do I care, Your kiss-es are worth wait-in'

for, be - lieve me. I don't stay out late,

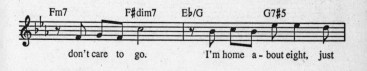

don't care to go. I'm home a-bout eight, just

me and my ra - di - o, ain't mis-be-hav-in'

I'm sav-in' my love for you. _____

ALL I ASK OF YOU
from THE PHANTOM OF THE OPERA

Music by ANDREW LLOYD WEBBER
Lyrics by CHARLES HART
Additional Lyrics by RICHARD STILGOE

Moderately slow

No more talk of dark-ness, for - get these wide-eyed fears: I'm

here, noth-ing can harm you, my words will warm and calm you.

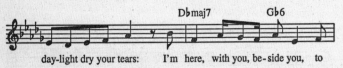

Let me be your free - dom; let

day-light dry your tears: I'm here, with you, be-side you, to

guard you and to guide you. Say you love me ev-'ry

wak - ing mo-ment; turn my head with talk of

Ebm7   **Ebm7/Ab**   **Db**   **Bbm7**

sum-mer-time.   Say   you   need me with you

Ebm7   **Ab**   **Db/F**   **Gb**

now   and   al-ways;   pro-mise me   that all you say is

Db/Ab   **Ebm/Ab**   **Ab6**   **Ebm/Ab**

true;   that's all   I   ask   of

Db
RAOUL:

you.
Let me be your shel-ter;   let me be your light.   You're

Dbmaj7   **Gb6**   **Cb**   **Ab/C**

safe;   no one will find you;   your fears are far   be-hind you.

Db
CHRISTINE:

All   I   want   is   free - dom,   a

Dbmaj7   **Gb6**

world with no more night;   and   you,   al-ways be-side me, to

RAOUL:

hold me and to hide me. Then say you'll share with me one

love, one life-time; let me lead you from your

so-li-tude. ___ Say you need me with you,

here be-side you. An-y-where you go, let me go

too. Chris-tine, that's all I ask of

CHRISTINE:
you.
Say you'll share with me one love, one life-time;

say the word and I will fol-low you. ___

ALWAYS TRUE TO YOU IN MY FASHION

from KISS ME, KATE

Words and Music by
COLE PORTER

If a cus-tom tail-ored vet ___ Asks me
hi-o, Mis-ter Thorne ___ Calls me

out for some-thing wet, ___ When the
up from night 'til morn, ___ Mis-ter

vet be-gins to pet ___ I cry "Hoo-ray!"
Thorne once cor-nered corn ___ and that ain't hay, ___

But I'm al-ways true to you, ___
But I'm al-ways true to you,

___ dar-lin', in my fash-ion, Yes, I'm
___ dar-lin', in my fash-ion, Yes, I'm

al-ways true to you, ___ dar-lin', in my way. ___
al-ways true to you, ___ dar-lin', in my way. ___

ANOTHER OP'NIN', ANOTHER SHOW

from KISS ME, KATE

Words and Music by
COLE PORTER

22

Four weeks___ you re - hearse and re - hearse.__

___ Three weeks ___ and it

could - n't be worse ___ One week _

___ will it ev - er be right? ___ Then

out o' the hat, ___ it's that big first night!

___ The o - ver - ture ___ is a -

bout to start. ___ You cross your fin -

AND THIS IS MY BELOVED

from KISMET

Words and Music by ROBERT WRIGHT
and GEORGE FORREST
(Music Based on Themes of A. BORODIN)

Slowly

Dawn's ___ prom-is-ing skies, ___
Strange ___ spice from the south, ___

pet-als on a pool ___ drift-ing; ___ i-
hon-ey thru the comb ___ sift-ing; ___ i-

mag-ine these ___ in one pair of eyes, ___
mag-ine these ___ in one ea-ger mouth, ___

1.
and this is my ___ be-lov-ed. ___

2.
and this is my ___ be-lov-ed. ___

And when she speaks, and when she talks to me,

ANY DREAM WILL DO

from JOSEPH AND THE AMAZING TECHNICOLOR® DREAMCOAT

Music by ANDREW LLOYD WEBBER
Lyrics by TIM RICE

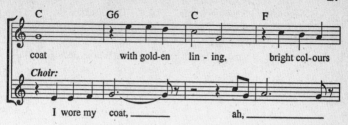

coat with gold-en lin - ing, bright col-ours

Choir:

I wore my coat, _____ ah, _____

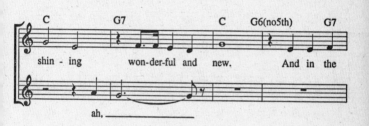

shin - ing won-der-ful and new, And in the

ah, _____

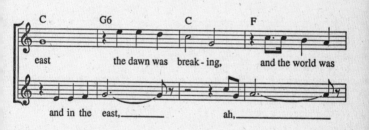

east the dawn was break - ing, and the world was

and in the east, _____ ah, _____

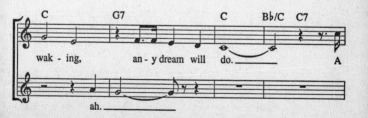

wak - ing, an - y dream will do. _____

A

ah. _____

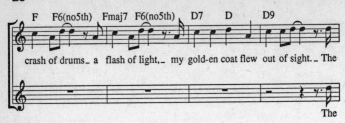

crash of drums_ a flash of light,_ my gold-en coat flew out of sight._ The

The

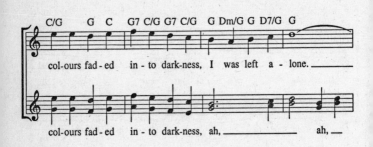

col-ours fad-ed in-to dark-ness, I was left a-lone._____

col-ours fad-ed in-to dark-ness, ah,_____ ah,_

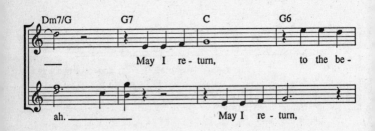

May I re-turn, to the be-

ah._____ May I re-turn,

gin-ning, the light is dim-ming and the dream is

ah,_____ ah._____

ANYONE CAN WHISTLE

from ANYONE CAN WHISTLE

Words and Music by
STEPHEN SONDHEIM

Slow and tenderly

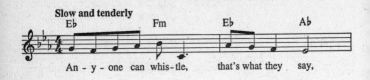

An-y-one can whis-tle, that's what they say,

eas-y. ___ An-y-one can whis-tle,

an-y old day, eas-y. ___ It's

all so sim-ple: Re-lax, let go, let fly! So

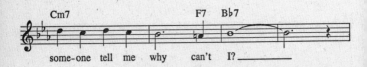

some-one tell me why can't I? ___

ANYTHING YOU CAN DO

from the Stage Production ANNIE GET YOUR GUN

Words and Music by
IRVING BERLIN

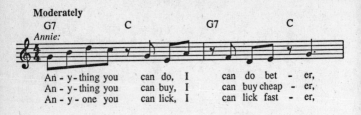

An - y - thing you can do, I can do bet - er,
An - y - thing you can buy, I can buy cheap - er,
An - y - one you can lick, I can lick fast - er,

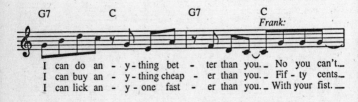

I can do an - y - thing bet - ter than you. No you can't.
I can buy an - y - thing cheap - er than you. Fif - ty cents.
I can lick an - y - one fast - er than you. With your fist.

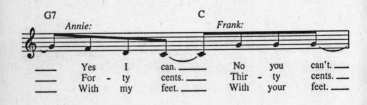

—— Yes I can. No you can't.
—— For - ty cents. Thir - ty cents.
—— With my feet. With your feet.

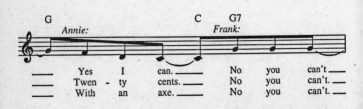

—— Yes I can. No you can't
—— Twen - ty cents. No you can't.
—— With an axe. No you can't.

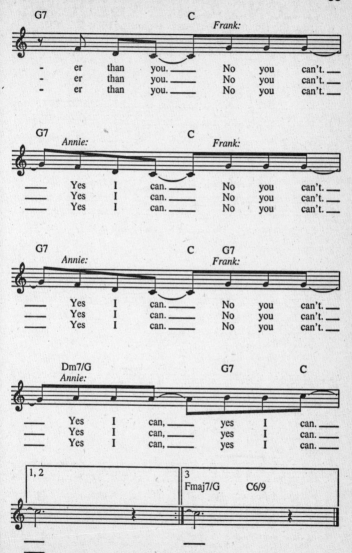

AS LONG AS HE NEEDS ME
from the Columbia Pictures - Romulus Film OLIVER!
Words and Music by
LIONEL BART

Slowly

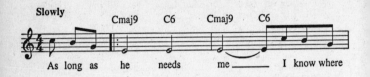

As long as he needs me _____ I know where

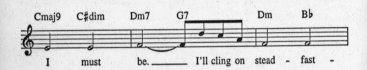

I must be. _____ I'll cling on stead - fast -

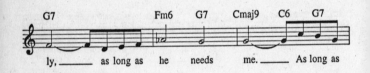

ly, _____ as long as he needs me. _____ As long as

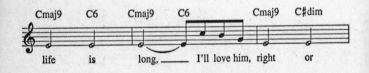

life is long, _____ I'll love him, right or

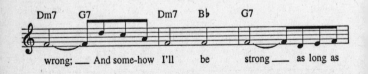

wrong; ___ And some-how I'll be strong ___ as long as

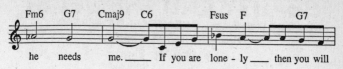

he   needs   me. ___   If you are lone - ly ___ then you will

know ___   When some-one   needs   you ___   you love them

so. ___   I won't be - tray   his   trust, ___ tho' peo-ple

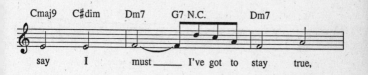

say   I   must ___ I've got to   stay   true,

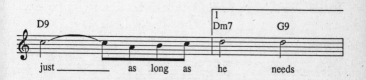

just ___   as   long   as   he   needs

me. ___   As long as   he   needs   me. ___

BEAUTY AND THE BEAST
from Walt Disney's BEAUTY AND THE BEAST:
THE BROADWAY MUSICAL

Lyrics by HOWARD ASHMAN
Music by ALAN MENKEN

BEING ALIVE
from COMPANY

Music and Lyrics by
STEPHEN SONDHEIM

Moderately

Some-bod - y hold me too close,
Some-bod - y need me too much,

Some-bod - y hurt me too deep,
Some-bod - y know me too well,

Some-bod - y sit in my chair, and ru-in my
Some-bod - y pull me up short and put me through

sleep, and make me a - ware of be-ing a -
hell, and give me sup - port for be-ing a -

live, _____ be-ing a - live. _____
live, _____ be-ing a -

live. _____ Make me a - live. _____ Make me con -

BEWITCHED
from PAL JOEY

Words by LORENZ HART
Music by RICHARD RODGERS

Moderately slow

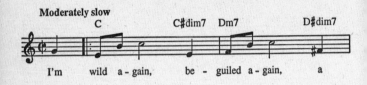

I'm wild a-gain, be-guiled a-gain, a

sim-per-ing, whim-per-ing child a-gain, be-

witched, both-ered and be-wild-ered am

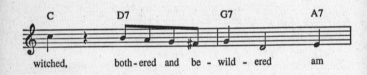

I.

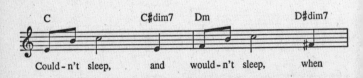

Could-n't sleep, and would-n't sleep, when

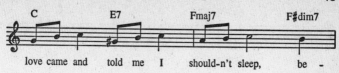

C   E7   Fmaj7   F#dim7

love came and   told me I   should-n't sleep,   be -

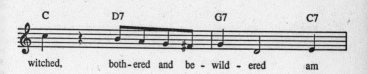

C   D7   G7   C7

witched,   both - ered and be - wild - ered   am

Fmaj7   A7

I.

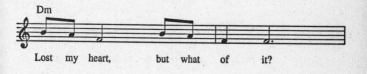

Dm

Lost   my   heart,   but what   of   it?

Am

He   is   cold   I   a - gree,

Dm   G7

he can laugh,   but I   love   it, _____ al - though the

44

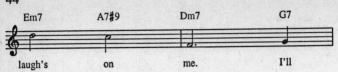

Em7   A7♯9   Dm7   G7

laugh's   on   me.   I'll

C   C♯dim7   Dm   D♯dim7

sing to him,   each   spring to him,   and

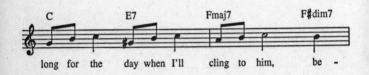

C   E7   Fmaj7   F♯dim7

long for the   day when I'll   cling to him,   be -

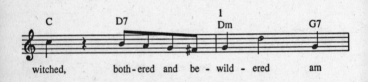

C   D7   1 Dm   G7

witched,   both-ered and be - wild - ered   am

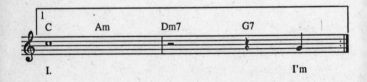

1
C   Am   Dm7   G7

I.   I'm

2
C   F   C

I. _____

BROTHERHOOD OF MAN
from HOW TO SUCCEED IN
BUSINESS WITHOUT REALLY TRYING

By FRANK LOESSER

There is a broth-er-hood of man.
A benev-o-lent broth-er-hood of man.
A no-ble tie that binds all hu-man hearts and minds in-to one broth-er-hood of man.
Your life-long broth-er-hood of man?

mem-ber-ship is free. Keep a-giv-ing each broth-er all you can. Oh aren't you proud to be in that fra-ter-ni-ty, the great big

BRING HIM HOME
from LES MISÉRABLES

Music by CLAUDE-MICHEL SCHÖNBERG
Lyrics by HERBERT KRETZMER and ALAIN BOUBLIL

BROADWAY BABY
from FOLLIES

Words and Music by
STEPHEN SONDHEIM

Swing

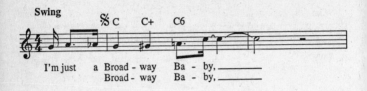

I'm just a Broad - way Ba - by, _____
Broad - way Ba - by, _____

walk - ing off my ti - red feet. ____
slav - ing at the five and ten. ____

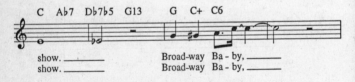

Pound - ing For - ty Sec - ond Street _____ to be in a
Dream - ing of the great day when _____ I'll be in a

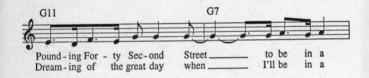

show. _____ Broad - way Ba - by, _____
show. _____ Broad - way Ba - by, _____

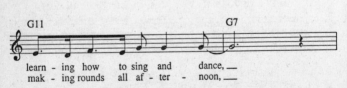

learn - ing how to sing and dance, __
mak - ing rounds all af - ter - noon, __

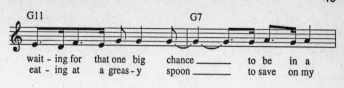

wait - ing for that one big chance _____ to be in a
eat - ing at a greas - y spoon _____ to save on my

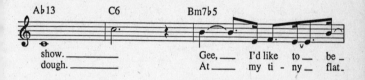

show. _____ Gee, _____ I'd like to _ be _
dough. _____ At _____ my ti - ny _ flat _

_____ on some mar - quee. _____ All _ twin -
_____ there's just my _ cat, _____ a _ bed _

_ kling _ lights, _ a spark _____ to pierce the _ dark _
_ and a chair. _ Still _____ I'll stick it _ till _

_____ from Bat - t'ry _ Park _____ to Wash -
_____ I'm on a _ bill _____ all o -

- ing - ton Heights _ some - day may - be, _____
- ver Times Square. _ Some - day may - be, _____

A7

Say, ___ Mis - ter Pro - duc - er, ___

B7

I'm ___ talk - in' to you, ___ sir, ___

C#9 **Eb9**

I don't need a lot, on - ly what I got,

D9 **G7#5** **D.S. al Coda**

plus a tube of grease-paint and a fol-low spot! ___ I'm a

CODA **Eb9 D9 Db9 D9 Eb9 E9 F9 G9**

I can get to strut my ___ stuff. ___

Ab13

Work-ing for a nice man like a Zieg-feld or a Weiss-man in a

D7b9 **G13** **C**

big time Broad - way show! ___

BRUSH UP
YOUR SHAKESPEARE
from KISS ME, KATE

Words and Music by
COLE PORTER

Brush up your Shake-speare,

start quot - ing him now. ___

Brush up your

Shake - speare, and the wom - en

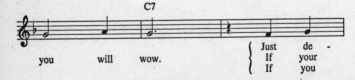

you will wow.

Just de -
If your
If you

54

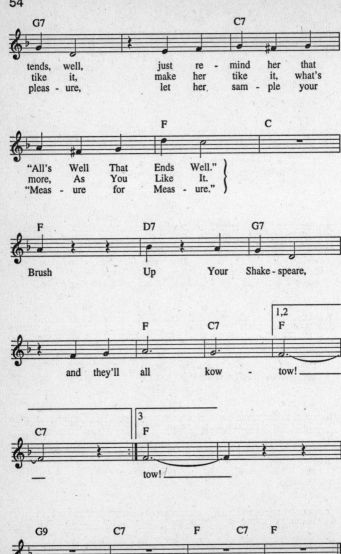

tends, well,   just re - mind her that
tike it,   make her tike it, what's
pleas - ure,   let her sam - ple your

"All's Well That Ends Well."
more, As You Like It.
"Meas - ure for Meas - ure."

Brush Up Your Shake - speare,

and they'll all kow - tow! ___

tow! ___

CAMELOT

from CAMELOT

Words by ALAN JAY LERNER
Music by FREDERICK LOEWE

1. A law was made a dis-tant moon a-
2., 3. win-ter is for-bid-den till De-

go here _____ Ju-ly and Au-gust
cem-ber _____ And ex-its March the

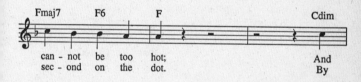

can-not be too hot; And
sec-ond on the dot. By

there's a le-gal lim-it to the
or-der sum-mer lin-gers through Sep-

snow here _____ in Cam-e-lot.
tem-ber _____ in

The Cam-e-lot.

Cam-e-lot!
Cam-e-lot!

Cam-e-lot!   I know it sounds a bit bi-
Cam-e-lot!   I know it gives a per-son

zarre,   But in Cam-e-lot,
pause,   But in Cam-e-lot,

Cam-e-lot,   That's
Cam-e-lot,   Those

how con-di-tions are.   The
are the le-gal laws.   The

rain may nev-er fall till af-ter sun-down. __
snow may nev-er slush up-on the hill-side. __

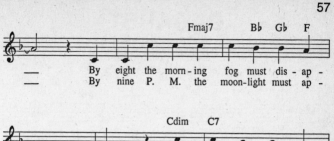

By eight the morn - ing fog must dis - ap -
By nine P. M. the moon-light must ap -

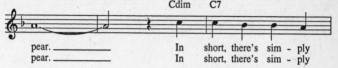

pear. _____ In short, there's sim - ply
pear. _____ In short, there's sim - ply

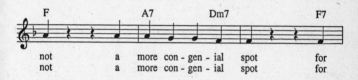

not a more con - gen - ial spot for
not a more con - gen - ial spot for

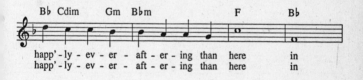

happ' - ly - ev - er - aft - er - ing than here in
happ' - ly - ev - er - aft - er - ing than here in

Cam - e - lot!
Cam - e -

The lot!

CABARET

from the Musical CABARET

Words by FRED EBB
Music by JOHN KANDER

2

Eb

ret.   Come   taste   the

Abm

wine.   Come   hear   the

Eb

band.   Come   blow   the

Cm   Cm#7   Cm7   F9

horn,   start   cel - e - brat - ing,

Bb7   **D.C. al Coda**

right   this   way,   your   ta - ble's   wait - ing.

CODA

Gm7   C9   Fm7

ret,   old   chum, __   come   to   the

Bb11   Eb

cab - a - ret. _____

CAN YOU FEEL
THE LOVE TONIGHT

Disney Presents THE LION KING:
THE BROADWAY MUSICAL

Music by ELTON JOHN
Lyrics by TIM RICE

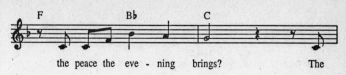

the peace the eve - ning brings? The

world, for once, _ in per - fect har-mo-ny___ with

all its liv - ing things. _ *Simba:* So

man - y things _ to tell _ her, but how to make _ her see the

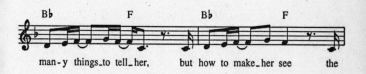

truth a-bout _ my past? _ Im-pos-si-ble. She'd turn a-way from me. *Nala:* He's

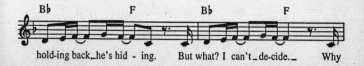

hold-ing back _ he's hid - ing. But what? I can't _ de-cide. _ Why

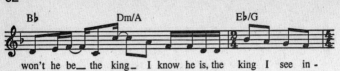

won't he be — the king — I know he is, the king I see in-

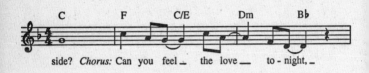

side? *Chorus:* Can you feel — the love — to - night, —

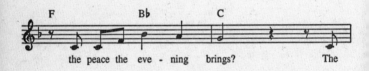

the peace the eve - ning brings? The

world, for once, — in per - fect har-mo-ny — with

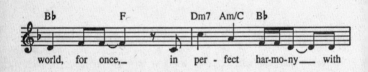

all its liv - ing things. — Can you feel — the love —

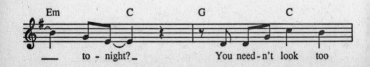

— to - night? — You need - n't look too

far.   Steal - ing through   the

night's un - cer-tain-ties,   love is where they are.__

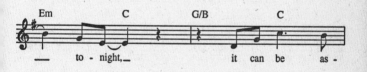

__   *Timon:* And if   he falls in love__

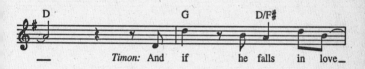

__ to - night,__   it can be as -

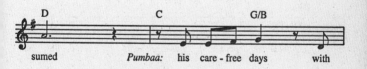

sumed   *Pumbaa:* his care - free days   with

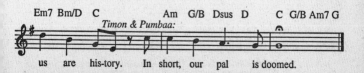

us are his-tory. In short, our pal   is doomed.

Timon & Pumbaa:

CLOSE EVERY DOOR

**from JOSEPH AND THE AMAZING
TECHNICOLOR® DREAMCOAT**

Music by ANDREW LLOYD WEBBER
Lyrics by TIM RICE

Espressivo

Joseph:

Close ev-'ry door to me, hide all the world from me,

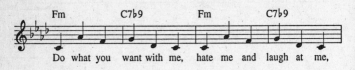

bar all the win-dows and shut out the light.

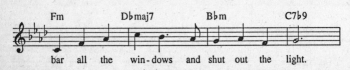

Do what you want with me, hate me and laugh at me,

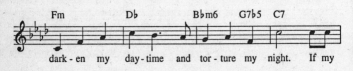

dark-en my day-time and tor-ture my night. If my

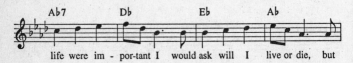

life were im-por-tant I would ask will I live or die, but

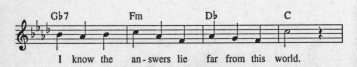

I know the an-swers lie far from this world.

Close ev - 'ry door to me, keep those I love from me.

Chil - dren of Is - rael are nev - er a - lone for I

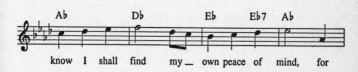

know I shall find my — own peace of mind, for

I have been prom - ised a land — of my

own. *Choir:* Close ev - 'ry door to me, hide all the

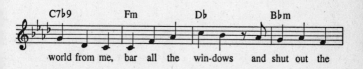

world from me, bar all the win-dows and shut out the

light. La la la la la la, la la la la la la,

la la la la la la la, la la la la la la la, la la la la la la la,

la la la la la la, la la la la la la la, la. *(Instrumental)*

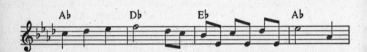

Joseph: Just

give me a num-ber in-stead of my name, for-

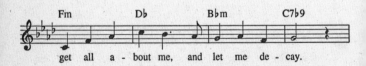

get all a-bout me, and let me de-cay.

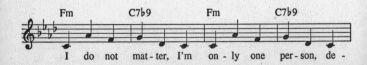

I do not mat-ter, I'm on-ly one per-son, de-

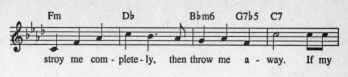

stroy me com‑plete‑ly, then throw me a‑way. If my

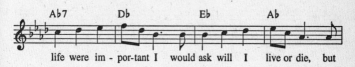

life were im‑por‑tant I would ask will I live or die, but

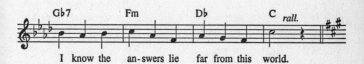

I know the an‑swers lie far from this world.

Slower

Close ev‑'ry door to me, keep those I love from me.

Chil‑dren of Is‑rael are nev‑er a‑lone, for we

know we shall find our __ own peace of mind, for

we have been prom‑ised, a land __ of our own.

COMEDY TONIGHT

**from A FUNNY THING HAPPENED
ON THE WAY TO THE FORUM**

Words and Music by
STEPHEN SONDHEIM

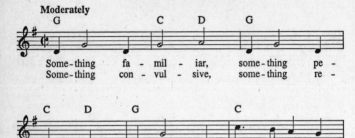

Some-thing fa-mil-iar, some-thing pe-
Some-thing con-vul-sive, some-thing re-

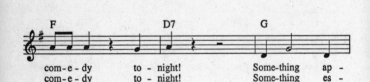

cul-iar, some-thing for ev-'ry-one, a
pul-sive, some-thing for ev-'ry-one, a

com-e-dy to-night! Some-thing ap-
com-e-dy to-night! Some-thing es-

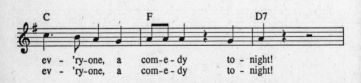

peal-ing, some-thing ap-pal-ling. Some-thing for
thet-ic, some-thing fre-net-ic. Some-thing for

ev-'ry-one, a com-e-dy to-night!
ev-'ry-one, a com-e-dy to-night!

CONSIDER YOURSELF
from the Columbia Pictures - Romulus Film OLIVER!

Words and Music by
LIONEL BART

DO I LOVE YOU BECAUSE YOU'RE BEAUTIFUL?

from CINDERELLA

Lyrics by OSCAR HAMMERSTEIN II
Music by RICHARD RODGERS

DO-RE-MI
from THE SOUND OF MUSIC

Lyrics by OSCAR HAMMERSTEIN II
Music by RICHARD RODGERS

Lively

Doe a deer, a fe - male deer,

Ray a drop of gol - den sun, ___

___ Me a name I

call my - self, Far a

long, long way to run. ___ Sew a

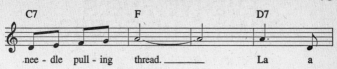

nee - dle pull - ing thread. _____ La a

note to fol - low sew, _____ Tea a

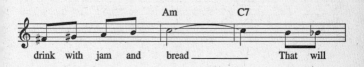

drink with jam and bread _____ That will

bring us back to do - oh - oh - oh!

do! _____ Do - re - mi -

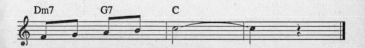

EVERYTHING'S COMING UP ROSES

from GYPSY

Words by STEPHEN SONDHEIM
Music by JULE STYNE

77

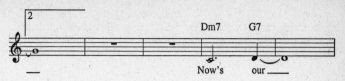

in - ning, _____ stand the world on its ear! _

_____ Set it _____ spin - ning, _

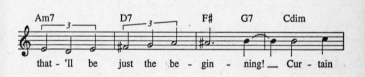

that - 'll be just the be - gin - ning! _ Cur - tain

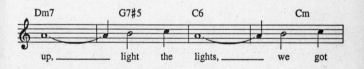

up, _____ light the lights, _____ we got

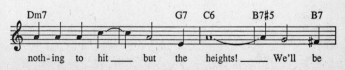

noth - ing to hit _____ but the heights! _____ We'll be

78

GONNA BUILD A MOUNTAIN

from the Musical Production
STOP THE WORLD – I WANT TO GET OFF

Words and Music by LESLIE BRICUSSE
and ANTHONY NEWLEY

Moderately bright

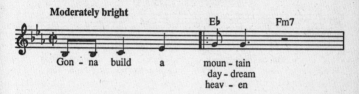

Gon - na build a moun - tain
day - dream
heav - en

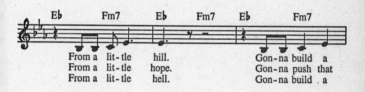

From a lit - tle hill. Gon - na build a
From a lit - tle hope. Gon - na push that
From a lit - tle hell. Gon - na build a

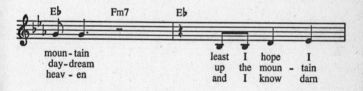

moun - tain least I hope I
day - dream up the moun - tain
heav - en and I know darn

will. Gon - na build a
slope. Gon - na build a
well, if I build my

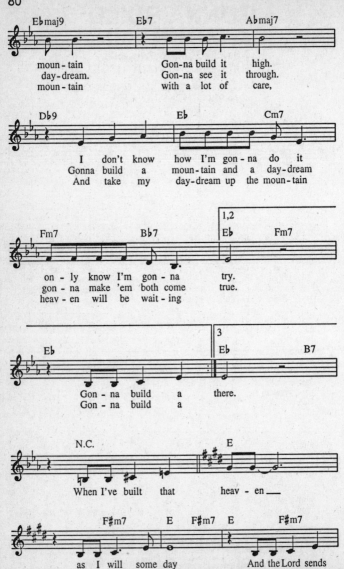

moun - tain
day - dream.
moun - tain

Gon-na build it high.
Gon-na see it through.
with a lot of care,

I don't know how I'm gon-na do it
Gonna build a moun-tain and a day-dream
And take my day-dream up the moun-tain

on - ly know I'm gon - na try.
gon - na make 'em both come true.
heav - en will be wait - ing

Gon - na build a there.
Gon - na build a

When I've built that heav - en __

as I will some day And the Lord sends

GET ME TO THE CHURCH ON TIME

from MY FAIR LADY

Words by ALAN JAY LERNER
Music by FREDERICK LOEWE

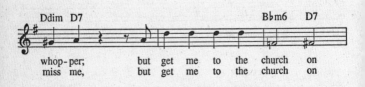

GETTING TO KNOW YOU

from THE KING AND I

Lyrics by OSCAR HAMMERSTEIN II
Music by RICHARD RODGERS

Moderately

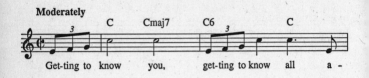

Get-ting to know you, get-ting to know all a-

bout you, _____ get-ting to like you

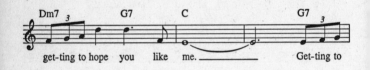

get-ting to hope you like me. _____ Get-ting to

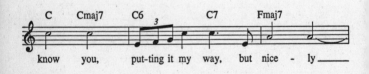

know you, put-ting it my way, but nice - ly _____

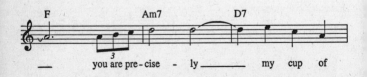

_____ you are pre - cise - ly _____ my cup of

HELLO, DOLLY!

from HELLO, DOLLY!
Music and Lyric by
JERRY HERMAN

band's   play - in' one   of   your old   fa - v'rite

songs from 'way back when.   So

{ take   her   wrap, fel - las,   find her an   emp - ty
{ gol - ly   gee,   fel - las,   find her a   va - cant

lap,   fel - las,} Dol - ly - 'll nev - er   go   a - way a-
knee, fel - las,}

gain!   Hel - go   a - way,

Dol - ly - 'll nev - er   go   a - way,   Dol - ly - 'll nev - er

go   a - way a - gain! _____

HELLO, YOUNG LOVERS

from THE KING AND I

Lyrics by OSCAR HAMMERSTEIN II
Music by RICHARD RODGERS

I COULD HAVE DANCED ALL NIGHT

from MY FAIR LADY

Words by ALAN JAY LERNER
Music by FREDERICK LOEWE

I DREAMED A DREAM
from LES MISÉRABLES

Music by CLAUDE-MICHEL SCHÖNBERG
Lyrics by HERBERT KRETZMER
Original Text by ALAIN BOUBLIL and JEAN-MARC NATEL

Moderately slow

I dreamed a dream in days gone by

when hope was high and life worth liv - ing. _____

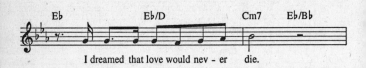

I dreamed that love would nev - er die.

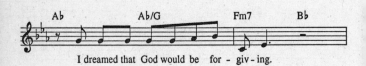

I dreamed that God would be for - giv - ing.

Then I was young and un - a - fraid

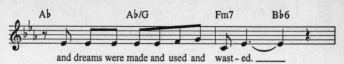

and dreams were made and used and wast-ed. ____

There was no ran-som to be paid,

no song un-sung no wine un-tast-ed.

But the ti-gers come at night

with their voic-es soft as thun-der.

As they tear your hope a-part,

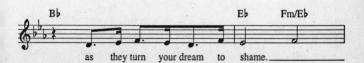

as they turn your dream to shame. ____

I ENJOY BEING A GIRL

from FLOWER DRUM SONG

Lyrics by OSCAR HAMMERSTEIN II
Music by RICHARD RODGERS

I GOT THE SUN
IN THE MORNING

from the Stage Production ANNIE GET YOUR GUN

Words and Music by
IRVING BERLIN

Medium jump tempo

Got no dia - mond, got no pearl,

still I think I'm a luck - y girl. I got the

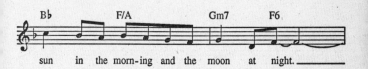

sun in the morn-ing and the moon at night.

Got no man - sion,

got no yacht, still I'm hap - py with

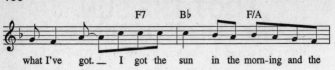

what I've got.__ I got the sun in the morn-ing and the

moon at night._____

Sun - shine _____ gives me a love -

- ly day. _____

Moon - light _____ gives me the milk -

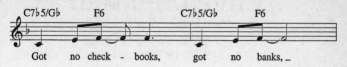

Got   no check - books,   got   no   banks, _

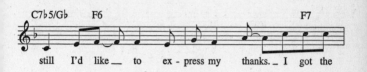

still   I'd   like __ to   ex - press my   thanks. _ I   got the

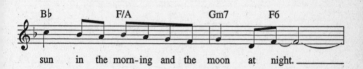

sun   in the morn-ing and the   moon   at   night. _____

_____   And   with   the

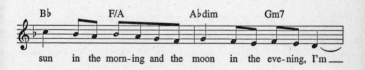

sun   in the morn-ing and the moon   in   the   eve-ning, I'm __

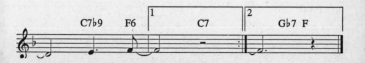

I HAVE DREAMED

from THE KING AND I

Lyrics by OSCAR HAMMERSTEIN II
Music by RICHARD RODGERS

I'VE GROWN ACCUSTOMED TO HER FACE

from MY FAIR LADY

Words by ALAN JAY LERNER
Music by FREDERICK LOEWE

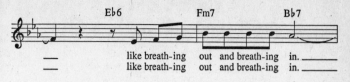

like breath-ing   out and breath-ing   in. _____
like breath-ing   out and breath-ing   in. _____

I was se - rene-ly   in - de-pen-dent and con -
I'm ver - y   grate-ful she's a wom-an and so

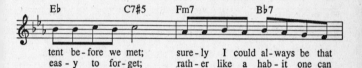

tent be - fore we met;   sure-ly   I could al-ways be that
eas - y to for-get;   rath - er like a hab - it one can

way a - gain and yet, I've grown ac - cus-tomed to her looks;   ac -
al-ways break and yet, I've grown ac - cus-tomed to the trace   of

cus-tomed to her voice;   ac - cus-tomed   to her
some-thing in the air;   ac - cus-tomed   to her

face.   I've grown ac - face.

IF EVER
I WOULD LEAVE YOU

from CAMELOT

Words by ALAN JAY LERNER
Music by FREDERICK LOEWE

Moderately, with expression

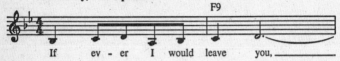

If ev - er I would leave you, ____

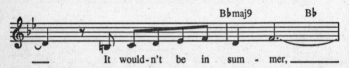

____ It would-n't be in sum - mer, ____

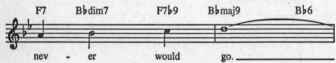

____ See - ing you in sum - mer I

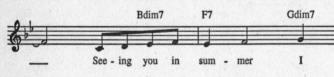

nev - er would go. ____

____ Your hair streaked with sun - light, ____

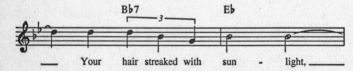

____ your lips red as flame, ____

your face with a lus - tre ____

that puts gold to shame! ____

But if I'd ev - er leave you, ____

it could-n't be in au - tumn, ____

how I'd leave in au - tumn I

nev - er will know. ____

I've seen how you spar - kle ____

IF I LOVED YOU

from CAROUSEL

Lyrics by OSCAR HAMMERSTEIN II
Music by RICHARD RODGERS

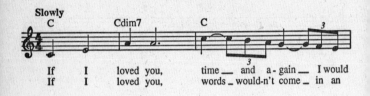

If   I   loved you,   time __ and a‑gain __ I would
If   I   loved you,   words __ would‑n't come __ in an

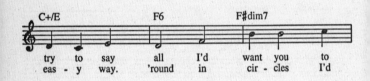

try   to   say   all   I'd   want you   to
eas - y   way.   'round   in   cir - cles   I'd

know. _____   go.

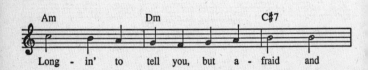

Long - in'   to   tell   you,   but a - fraid   and

shy,   I'd   let   my   gold - en   chanc - es

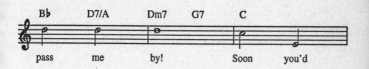

pass   me   by!   Soon   you'd

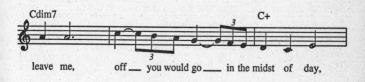

leave me,   off ___ you would go ___ in the midst of   day,

nev - er,   nev - er   to   know _____

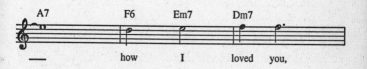

_____   how   I   loved you,

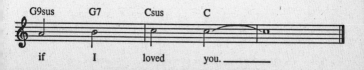

if   I   loved   you. _____

THE IMPOSSIBLE DREAM
(The Quest)
from MAN OF LA MANCHA

Lyric by JOE DARION
Music by MITCH LEIGH

IT'S THE HARD-KNOCK LIFE
from the Musical Production ANNIE
Lyric by MARTIN CHARNIN
Music by CHARLES STROUSE

Moderately

It's the hard – knock life for us!
nev – er see,

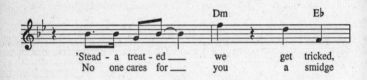

It's the hard – knock life for us!
San – ta Claus, what's that? Who's he?

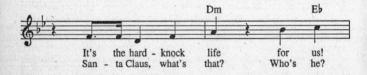

'Stead – a treat – ed ___ we get tricked,
No one cares for ___ you a smidge

'stead – a kiss – es ___ we get kicked,
when you're in an ___ or – phan – ige }

To Coda ⊕

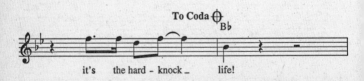

it's the hard – knock ___ life!

Got no folks to speak of, so, ___ it's the hard-knock
row we hoe. ___ Cot - ton blan - kets ___
'stead - a wool, ___ emp - ty bel - lies ___
'stead - a full, ___ it's the hard - knock ___
life. Don't it feel like the wind is al-ways
howl - in'? Don't it seem like there's nev - er an - y
light? Once a day don't you want to throw the
towel in? It's eas - i - er than put-tin' up a

116

fight. No one's there when your dreams at night get

creep-y. ___ No one cares if you grow, or if you

shrink. No one dries when your eyes get wet and

weep-y. ___ From the cry-in' you would think this place would

D.S. al Coda

sink. Oh! San - ta Claus we

CODA

life! (Yes it is) ___ It's the hard - knock

life. (Yes it is) ___ It's the hard-knock life.

THE LAST NIGHT OF THE WORLD
from MISS SAIGON
Music by CLAUDE-MICHEL SCHÖNBERG
Lyrics by RICHARD MALTBY JR. and ALAIN BOUBLIL
Adapted from original French Lyrics by ALAIN BOUBLIL

so - lo sax - o - phone, ___ it's

tell - ing me ___ to hold you tight __ and

dance like it's the last ___ night of the world.

CHRIS: On the oth-er side of the earth __

there's a place where life still has worth. __ I will

take you. KIM: I'll go with you. __

CHRIS: You won't be - lieve all the things you'll see. __

__ I know 'cause you'll see them all with me. __

CHRIS:

KIM: If we're to - geth - er, well then, we'll

120

LOSING MY MIND
from FOLLIES
Words and Music by
STEPHEN SONDHEIM

Slow and free

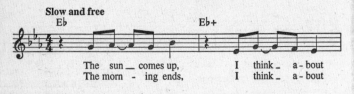

The sun __ comes up, I think __ a-bout
The morn - ing ends, I think __ a-bout

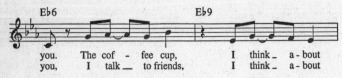

you. The cof - fee cup, I think __ a-bout
you, I talk __ to friends, I think __ a-bout

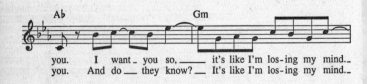

you. I want __ you so, _____ it's like I'm los-ing my mind. __
you. And do __ they know? __ It's like I'm los-ing my mind. __

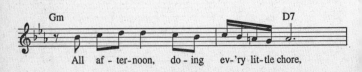

All af - ter-noon, do - ing ev-'ry lit-tle chore,

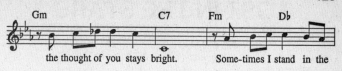

the thought of you stays bright. Some-times I stand in the

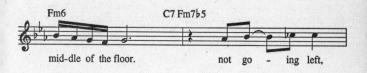

mid-dle of the floor. not go - ing left,

not go - ing right. I dim __ the lights

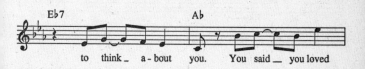

and think __ a - bout you, spend sleep - less nights

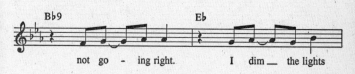

to think __ a - bout you. You said __ you loved

me, or were you just be - ing kind? __

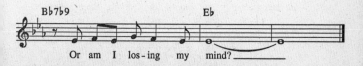

Or am I los - ing my mind? __

LOST IN THE STARS

from the Musical Production LOST IN THE STARS

Words by MAXWELL ANDERSON
Music by KURT WEILL

Moderately

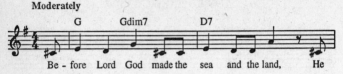

Be - fore Lord God made the sea and the land, He

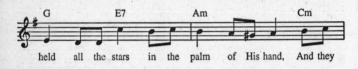

held all the stars in the palm of His hand, And they

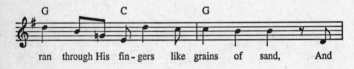

ran through His fin - gers like grains of sand, And

one lit - tle star fell a - lone. Then the

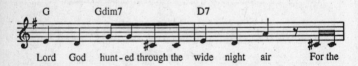

Lord God hunt - ed through the wide night air For the

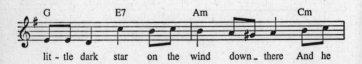

lit - tle dark star on the wind down _ there And he

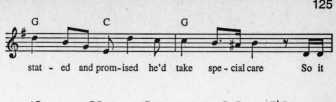

stat - ed and prom-ised he'd take spe - cial care So it

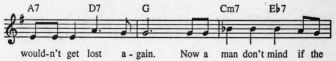

would-n't get lost a - gain. Now a man don't mind if the

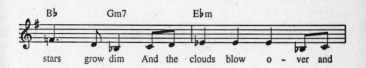

stars grow dim And the clouds blow o - ver and

dark - en him, So long as the Lord God's

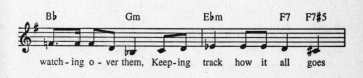

watch - ing o - ver them, Keep-ing track how it all goes

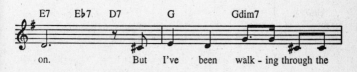

on. But I've been walk - ing through the

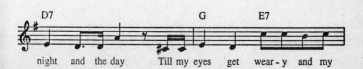

night and the day Till my eyes get wear-y and my

head turns _ gray, And _ some - times it seems may - be

God's gone a - way, For - get - ting the prom-ise that we

heard him say And we're lost out here in the stars,

Lit-tle stars, big stars, blow - ing through the night,

And we're lost out here in the stars,

Lit-tle stars, big stars, blow - ing through the night,

And we're lost out here in the stars. _____

LUCK BE A LADY
from GUYS AND DOLLS

By FRANK LOESSER

I know the way you've treat-ed oth-er guys you've

been with luck be a la-dy with me. ___

A la-dy does-n't leave her

es-cort. ___ It is-n't fair ___

___ it is-n't nice. ___ A

la-dy does-n't wan-der all o-ver the

LOVE, LOOK AWAY

from FLOWER DRUM SONG

Lyrics by OSCAR HAMMERSTEIN II
Music by RICHARD RODGERS

Moderately, with expression

Love, look a - way! _____

Love, look a - way from me. Fly when you pass my

door, Fly and get lost at sea.

Call it a day. _____

Love, let us say we're through. No good are you for

me, No good am I for you.

MAME
from MAME

Music and Lyric by
JERRY HERMAN

You coax the blues right out __ of the horn,
You've brought the cake-walk back __ in-to style,

Mame. __ You charm the husk right off __ of the
Mame. __ You make the weep-in' wil - low tree

corn, Mame. __ You've got the
smile, Mame. __ Your skin is

ban - joes strum - min' and plunk-in' out a tune to beat the
Dix - ie sat - in, there's reb - el in your man - ner and your

band. The whole plan - ta-tion's hum - min' since
speech. You may be from Man - hat - tan, but

you brought Dix - ie back to Dix - ie-land. You make the
Geor - gia nev - er had a sweet-er peach. You make our

cot - ton eas - y to pick, Mame. _
black - eyed peas _ and our grits, Mame, _

You give my old mint ju - lep a kick,
seem like the bill of fare _ at the Ritz,

Mame. _ You make the old mag-no - lia tree
Mame. _ You came, you saw, you con - quered and

blos - som at the men - tion of your name.
ab - so-lute - ly noth - ing is the same.

You've made us feel a - live _ a-gain, you've giv - en
Your spe - cial fas - ci - na - tion-'ll prove to be

us the drive _ a-gain, to make the South re-vive _ a-gain,
in - spi-ra - tion-al, we think you're just sen-sa - tion-al,

1
C Cdim7 Dm7 G7

2
C

Mame. Mame. _____

MEMORY

from CATS

Music by ANDREW LLOYD WEBBER
Text by TREVOR NUNN after T.S. ELIOT

Freely

Mid-night. _ Not a sound from the pave - ment. _ Has the moon lost her

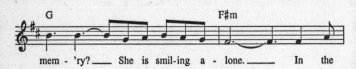

mem - 'ry? ____ She is smil-ing a - lone. ____ In the

lamp-light the with - ered leaves col - lect at my feet And the

wind ____ be - gins to moan.

Mem - 'ry. _ All a-lone in the moon - light _ I can smile at the

old days, _ I was beau - ti-ful then. ____ I re -

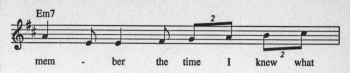

mem - ber   the   time   I   knew   what

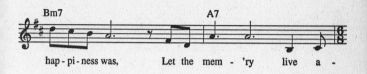

hap - pi - ness was,   Let the mem - 'ry   live a -

gain.   Ev - 'ry street   lamp

seems _____   to   beat _____   a

fa - tal - is - tic _____   warn - ing.

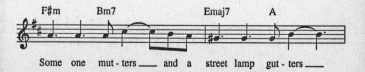

Some one mut - ters _____ and a street lamp gut - ters _____

and soon it will be morn - ing ___ Day - light. ___ I must wait for the sun - rise. ___ I must think of a new life ___ And I must-n't give in. ___ When the dawn comes to-night will be a mem-o-ry too And a new day will ___ be - gin.

Burnt out ends of smok - y days ___ the stale cold smell ___ of ___ morn - ing The

138

THE MUSIC OF THE NIGHT
from THE PHANTOM OF THE OPERA

Music by ANDREW LLOYD WEBBER
Lyrics by CHARLES HART
Additional Lyrics by RICHARD STILGOE

Moderately slow

Night - time sharp - ens, height-ens each sen - sa - tion;
Slow - ly, gent - ly night un-furls its splen - dor;
Float - ing, fall - ing, sweet in-tox - i - ca - tion.

dark - ness stirs and wakes i - mag - i - na - tion.
grasp it sense it, trem - u - lous and ten - der.
Touch me, trust me, sa - vour each sen - sa - tion.

To Coda ⊕

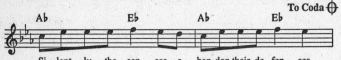

Si - lent - ly the sen - ses a - ban-don their de - fen - ses.
Turn your face a - way from the gar-ish light of day, turn your
Let the dream be - gin, let your dark - er side give in to the

(Instrumental)

thoughts a - way from cold, un - feel - ing light and

lis-ten to the mu-sic of the night. Close your

eyes and sur-ren-der to your dark-est dreams! Purge your

thoughts of the life you knew be - fore! Close your

eyes, let your spir-it start to soar, and you'll

live as you've nev-er lived be-fore.

Soft-ly, deft-ly, mu-sic shall ca-ress you.

Hear it, feel it, se-cret-ly pos-sess you.

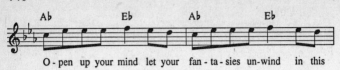

O - pen up your mind let your fan - ta - sies un-wind in this

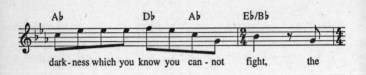

dark-ness which you know you can - not fight, the

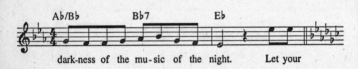

dark-ness of the mu - sic of the night. Let your

mind start a jour - ney through a

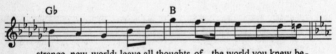

strange, new world; leave all thoughts of the world you knew be-

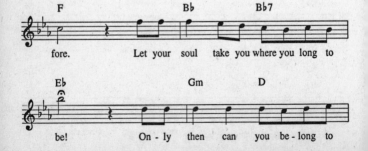

fore. Let your soul take you where you long to

be! On - ly then can you be - long to

CODA

me.

pow-er of the mu-sic that I write, the pow-er of the music of the night. *(Instrumental)*

You a-lone can make my song take flight,

help me make the mu-sic of the night. _____

MY FAVORITE THINGS

from THE SOUND OF MUSIC

Lyrics by OSCAR HAMMERSTEIN II
Music by RICHARD RODGERS

Lively, with spirit

Rain - drops on ros - es and whis - kers on
Cream col - ored po - nies and crisp ap - ple

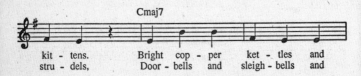

kit - tens. Bright cop - per ket - tles and
stru - dels, Door - bells and sleigh - bells and

warm wool - en mit - tens, Brown pa - per
schnitz - el with noo - dles, Wild geese that

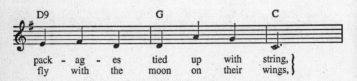

pack - ag - es tied up with string,}
fly with the moon on their wings,}

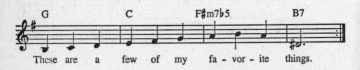

These are a few of my fa - vor - ite things.

E

Girls in white

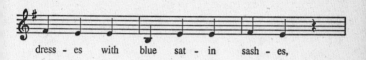

dress - es with blue sat - in sash - es,

A

Snow - flakes that stay on my nose and eye -

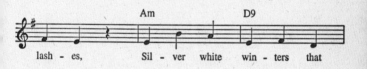

Am   D9

lash - es,   Sil - ver white win - ters that

G   C   G

melt in - to springs,   These are a

C   F#m7b5   B7

few of my fa - vor - ite things.

When the dog bites,   When the

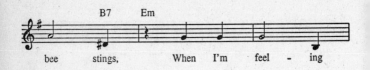

bee stings,   When I'm feel - ing

sad, _____ I sim - ply re - mem - ber my

fa - vor - ite things and then I don't

feel   so

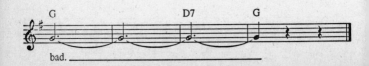

bad. _____

MY SHIP

from the Musical Production LADY IN THE DARK
Words by IRA GERSHWIN
Music by KURT WEILL

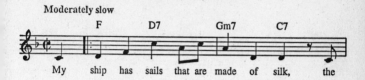

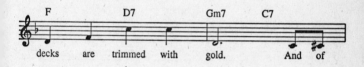

bin;   the   sun   sits   high   in   a

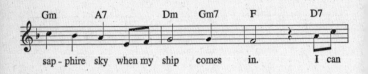

sap - phire   sky   when my   ship   comes   in.   I   can

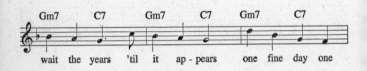

wait   the   years   'til   it   ap - pears   one   fine   day   one

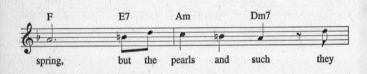

spring,   but   the   pearls   and   such   they

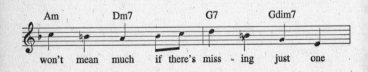

won't   mean   much   if there's   miss - ing   just   one

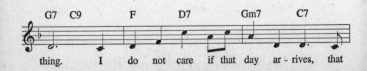

thing.   I   do   not   care   if that   day   ar - rives, that

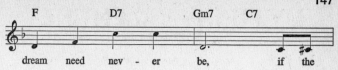

dream   need   nev - er   be,   if the

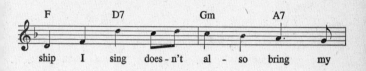

ship   I   sing   does - n't   al - so   bring   my

own   true   love   to   me.   My

own   true   love   to   me,   if the

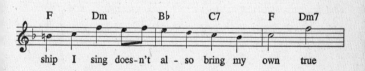

ship   I   sing does-n't al - so bring my   own   true

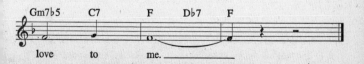

love   to   me. _____

MY FUNNY VALENTINE

from BABES IN ARMS

Words by LORENZ HART
Music by RICHARD RODGERS

My fun-ny val-en-tine, sweet com-ic

val-en-tine, you make me smile with my

heart. _____ Your looks are laugh-a-ble,

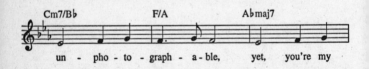

un-pho-to-graph-a-ble, yet, you're my

fav-'rite work of art. _____ Is your

MY ROMANCE
from JUMBO

Words by LORENZ HART
Music by RICHARD RODGERS

Moderately slow

My ro - mance does-n't have to have a moon in the sky, my ro - mance does-n't need a blue la - goon stand-ing by; no month of May, no twin - kling stars, no hide a - way, no soft gui -

Em7 A7 Dmaj7 Em7

tars. My ro - mance does - n't

F#m7 Fdim7 Em7 A7

need a cas - tle ris - ing in

Dmaj7 C13 Bm Bm(maj7)

Spain, nor a dance to a

Bm7 B7 Em7 A7

con - stant - ly sur - pris - ing re -

Dmaj7 D7 Gmaj7 Gmaj7/F# Em7 Em7/D

frain. Wide a - wake I can make my most fan -

C#7 C9#11 Bm7 Bb9 Dmaj7/6 Bm7

tas - tic dreams come true; my ro - mance does-n't

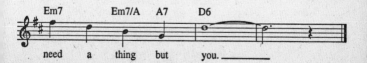

Em7 Em7/A A7 D6

need a thing but you. _____

OH, WHAT A BEAUTIFUL MORNIN'

from OKLAHOMA!

Lyrics by OSCAR HAMMERSTEIN II
Music by RICHARD RODGERS

Bright Waltz

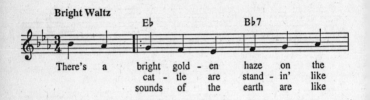

There's a bright gold — en haze on the
cat — tle are stand — in' like
sounds of the earth are like

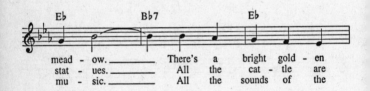

mead — ow. _____ There's a bright gold — en
stat — ues. _____ All the cat — tle are
mu — sic. _____ All the sounds of the

haze on the mead — ow. _____ The
stand — in' like stat — ues. _____ They
earth are like mu — sic. _____ The

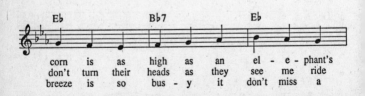

corn is as high as an el — e — phant's
don't turn their heads as they see me ride
breeze is so bus — y it don't miss a

OKLAHOMA
from OKLAHOMA!

Lyrics by OSCAR HAMMERSTEIN II
Music by RICHARD RODGERS

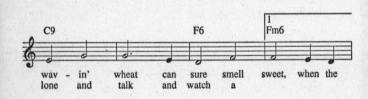

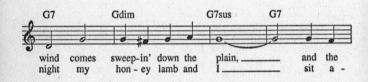

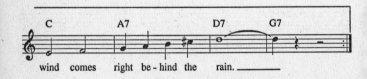

hawk mak - in' la - zy cir - cles in the sky. ___ We know we be - long to the land ___ and the land we be - long to is grand! ___ And when we say ___ Yeeow! A - yip - i - o - ee - ay! ___ We're on - ly say - in' you're do - in' fine, O - kla - ho - ma! O - kla - ho - ma ___ O. K. ___

ON MY OWN
from LES MISÉRABLES

Music by CLAUDE-MICHEL SCHÖNBERG
Lyrics by ALAIN BOUBLIL, HERBERT KRETZMER, JOHN CAIRD,
TREVOR NUNN and JEAN-MARC NATEL

Moderately slow

EPONINE:

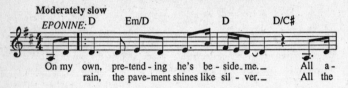

On my own, pre-tend-ing he's be-side me.__ All a-
rain, the pave-ment shines like sil - ver.__ All the

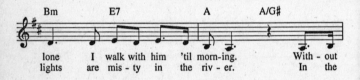

lone I walk with him 'til morn-ing. With - out
lights are mis-ty in the riv-er. In the

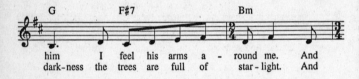

him I feel his arms a - round me. And
dark-ness the trees are full of star-light. And

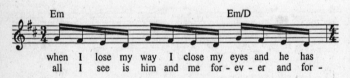

when I lose my way I close my eyes and he has
all I see is him and me for - ev - er and for -

1.
found me. In the

2.
ev - er. And I

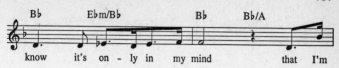

know it's on – ly in my mind that I'm

talk – ing to my – self and not to him. And al –

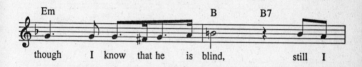

though I know that he is blind, still I

say there's a way for us. I

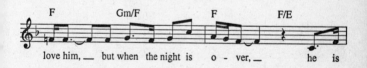

love him, __ but when the night is o – ver, __ he is

gone, the riv – er's just a riv – er. With –

out him the world a-round me chang – es. The

trees are bare and ev - 'ry-where the streets are full of stran-gers.

I love him ___ but ev - 'ry day I'm learn - ing ___ all my life I've on - ly been pre-tend - ing. ___

With-out me his world will go on turn - ing. ___ The world is full of hap - pi - ness that I have nev - er known.

I love him, _ I love him, _ I love him, ___ but on - ly on my own.

PEOPLE
from FUNNY GIRL

Words by BOB MERRILL
Music by JULE STYNE

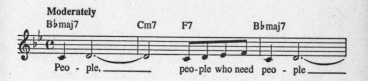

Moderately

Peo - ple, _____ peo-ple who need peo - ple _____

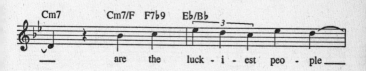

_____ are the luck - i - est peo - ple _____

_____ in the world. We're

chil - dren _____ need - ing oth - er

chil - dren _____ and yet

let - ting our grown - up pride hide all the need in -

side, act - ing more like chil - dren, than

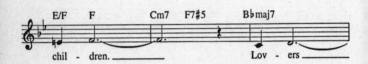

chil - dren. _____ Lov - ers _____

_____ are ver - y spe - cial peo - ple, _____

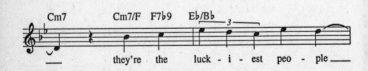

_____ they're the luck - i - est peo - ple _____

_____ in the world. _____ With one

per - son, _____ one ver - y spe - cial

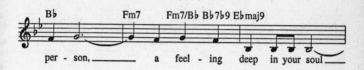

per - son, _____ a feel - ing deep in your soul _____

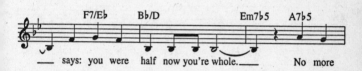

_____ says: you were half now you're whole. _____ No more

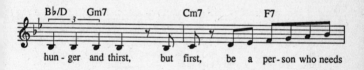

hun - ger and thirst, but first, be a per - son who needs

peo - ple, _____ peo-ple who need peo - ple _____

_____ are the luck - i - est peo - ple

in the world. _____

ON THE STREET WHERE YOU LIVE

from MY FAIR LADY

Words by ALAN JAY LERNER
Music by FREDERICK LOEWE

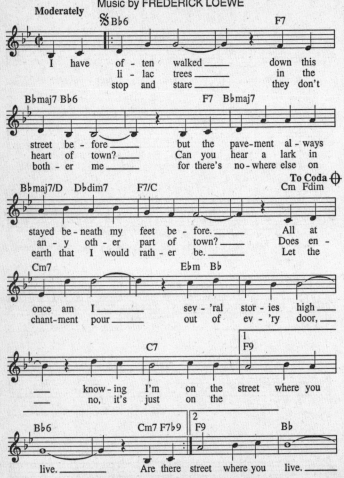

I have of-ten walked down this
li-lac trees in the
stop and stare they don't

street be-fore but the pave-ment al-ways
heart of town? Can you hear a lark in
both-er me for there's no-where else on

stayed be-neath my feet be-fore. All at
an-y oth-er part of town? Does en-
earth that I would rath-er be. Let the

once am I sev-'ral stor-ies high
chant-ment pour out of ev-'ry door,

know-ing I'm on the street where you
no, it's just on the

live. Are there street where you live.

ONE
from A CHORUS LINE

Music by MARVIN HAMLISCH
Lyric by EDWARD KLEBAN

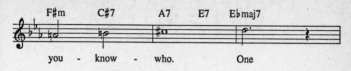

you - know - who. One

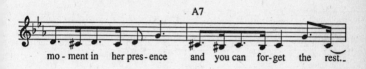

mo - ment in her pres - ence and you can for-get the rest...

For the girl is sec-ond best __ to

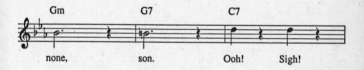

none, son. Ooh! Sigh!

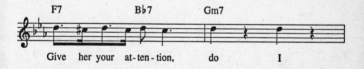

Give her your at - ten - tion, do I

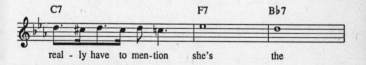

real - ly have to men-tion she's the

one? _____

PEOPLE WILL SAY WE'RE IN LOVE
from OKLAHOMA!

Lyrics by OSCAR HAMMERSTEIN II
Music by RICHARD RODGERS

Moderately

Don't throw ____ bou - quets at me, ____

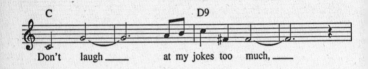

don't please ____ my folks too much. ____

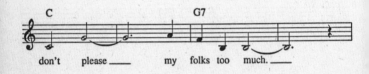

Don't laugh ____ at my jokes too much, ____

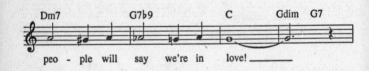

peo - ple will say we're in love!

Don't sigh ____ and gaze at me,

your sighs ___ are so like mine. ___

Your eyes ___ must-n't glow like mine, ___

peo - ple will say we're in love! ___

Don't start ___ col - lect - ing things, ___

give me my rose and my glove. ___

Sweet - heart, ___ they're sus - pect - ing things, ___

peo - ple will say we're in love. ___

THE PHANTOM OF THE OPERA

from THE PHANTOM OF THE OPERA
Music by ANDREW LLOYD WEBBER
Lyrics by CHARLES HART
Additional Lyrics by RICHARD STILGOE and MIKE BATT

Bb · Ab Bb Dbdim7 · Gm · *PHANTOM:*

(Instrumental) · Sing once a-

Csus Cm F · Gm

gain with me ____ our strange du-et; ____ my pow-er

Csus Cm F · Gm

o-ver you ____ grows strong-er yet. · And though you

Ebmaj7 Cm/Eb F · Gm

turn from me ____ to glance be-hind, ____ the

Gm

Phan - tom of the op-er-a is

Cdim7 F#dim7 · Gm · F#m Fm E

there ____ in-side your mind. ____ *(Instrumental)*

Eb D D7 Em · *CHRISTINE:*

Those who have

Asus Am D/F# · Em/B

seen your face ____ draw back in fear. ____ I am the

Asus Am D/F# · *PHANTOM:* · Em/B

mask you wear, ____ it's me they hear.

A PRETTY GIRL
IS LIKE A MELODY

from the 1919 Stage Production ZIEGFELD FOLLIES

Words and Music by
IRVING BERLIN

Moderately

A pret-ty girl _____ is like a

mel - o - dy _____ that haunts you

night and day. _____

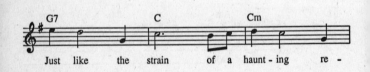

Just like the strain of a haunt-ing re-

frain, she'll start up-on a mar-a-thon and

SEASONS OF LOVE
from RENT

Words and Music by
JONATHAN LARSON

Moderately

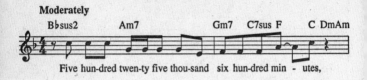

Five hun-dred twen-ty five thou-sand six hun-dred min - utes,

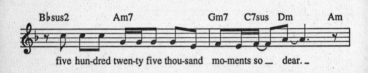

five hun-dred twen-ty five thou-sand mo-ments so _ dear. _

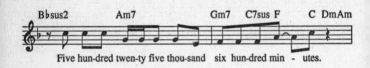

Five hun-dred twen-ty five thou-sand six hun-dred min - utes.

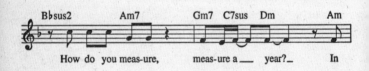

How do you meas-ure, meas-ure a _ year? _ In

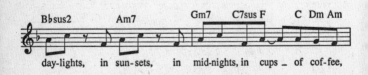

day-lights, in sun-sets, in mid-nights, in cups _ of cof-fee,

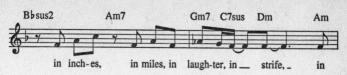

in inch-es, in miles, in laugh-ter, in __ strife, __ in

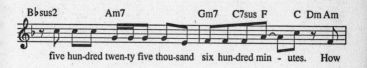

five hun-dred twen-ty five thou-sand six hun-dred min - utes. How

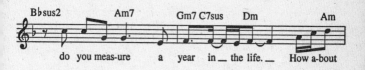

do you meas-ure a year in __ the life. __ How a-bout

love? _____ How a-bout

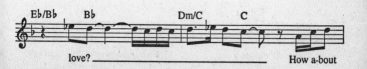

love? _____ How a-bout

love? _____ Meas-ure in

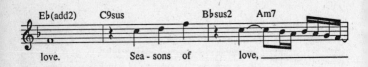

love.   Sea - sons of   love, _____

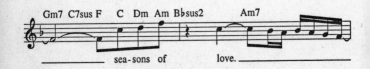

_____ sea-sons of   love. _____

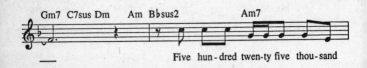

—   Five hun-dred twen-ty five thou-sand

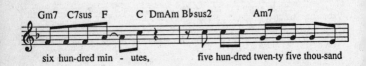

six hun-dred min - utes,   five hun-dred twen-ty five thou-sand

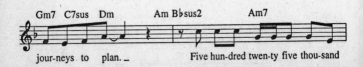

jour-neys to plan. _   Five hun-dred twen-ty five thou-sand

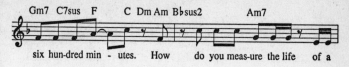

six hun-dred min - utes. How do you meas-ure the life of a

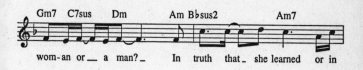

wom-an or __ a man? __ In truth that __ she learned or in

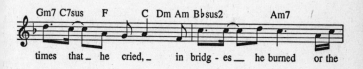

times that __ he cried, __ in bridg - es __ he burned or the

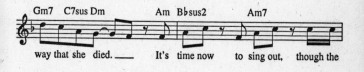

way that she died. ___ It's time now to sing out, though the

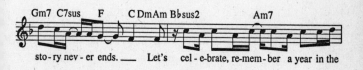

sto-ry nev-er ends. ___ Let's cel-e-brate, re-mem-ber a year in the

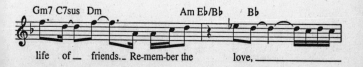

life of __ friends. __ Re-mem-ber the love, _____

178

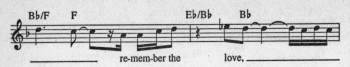

re-mem-ber the love,

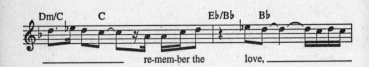

re-mem-ber the love,

meas-ure in love.

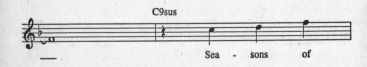

Sea - sons of

love, sea-sons of

love.

SOMEONE LIKE YOU

from JEKYLL & HYDE

Words by LESLIE BRICUSSE
Music by FRANK WILDHORN

Slowly

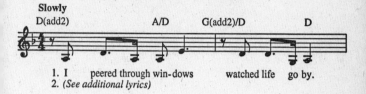

1. I peered through win-dows watched life go by.
2. *(See additional lyrics)*

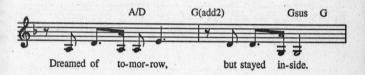

Dreamed of to-mor-row, but stayed in-side.

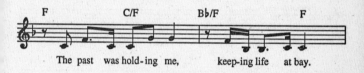

The past was hold-ing me, keep-ing life at bay.

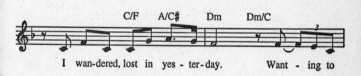

I wan-dered, lost in yes-ter-day. Want - ing to

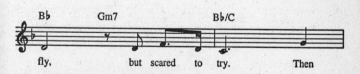

fly, but scared to try. Then

Chorus

Some - one _ like you found some - one _ like me. And
sud - den - ly ____ noth - ing is the same. My
heart's tak - en wing, _ and I feel so a - live, _ 'cause
some - one like you ____ found me.
some - one like you ____ found
me. Oh, ____ some - one _ like you found
some - one _ like me. And sud - den - ly ____ noth - ing will

ev - er   be the same.   My heart's tak - en wing,___   and I

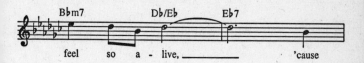

feel   so   a - live,_____   'cause

Slowly, freely

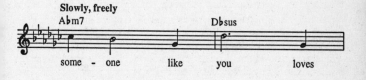

some - one   like   you   loves

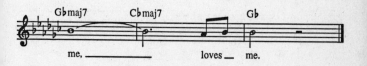

me,_____   loves ___ me.

Additional Lyrics

2. It's like you took my dreams, made each one real,
   You reached inside of me and made me feel.
   And now I see a world I've never seen before.
   Your love has opened every door;
   You've set me free, now I can soar.

Chorus: For someone like you found someone like me.
   You touched my heart, nothing is the same.
   There's a new way to live, a new way to love,
   'Cause someone like you found me.

SEPTEMBER SONG
from the Musical Play KNICKERBOCKER HOLIDAY

Words by MAXWELL ANDERSON
Music by KURT WEILL

Male: When I was a young man court-ing the girls I
Female: When you meet with the young men ear-ly in spring they

played me a wait - ing game. If a
court you in song and rhyme. They

maid re-fused me with toss-ing curls I
woo you with words and a clo-ver ring, but

let the old earth take a cou-ple of whirls, while I
if you ex-am-ine the goods they bring they have

plied her with tears in lieu of pearls, and as
lit-tle to offer but the songs they sing, and a

time came a-round she came my way, as
plen-ti-ful waste of time of day, a

time came a-round she came. Oh, it's a
plen-ti-ful waste of time.

long, long while from May to De - cem - ber, __

but the days grow short, when you reach Sep -

tem - ber. __ When the au - tumn weath - er __

turns the leaves to flame one has-n't got

time for the wait-ing game. __ Oh, the

days dwin-dle down __ to a pre-cious few, __ Sep-

tem - ber, __ No - vem - ber! And these few

pre-cious days I'll spend with you, these pre-cious

days I'll spend with you. __

SEVENTY SIX TROMBONES
from Meredith Willson's THE MUSIC MAN

By MEREDITH WILLSON

Sev-en-ty six trom - bones led the big pa - rade, __
six trom - bones caught the morn - ing sun, __

__ with a hun-dred and ten cor - nets close at
__ with a hun-dred and ten cor - nets right be-

hand. _____ They were fol-lowed by rows and
hind. _____ There were more than a thou - sand

rows of the fin - est vir - tu - o - sos, the
reeds spring - ing up __ like __ weeds, there were

cream of ev - 'ry fa - mous band. _____

G7 | 2 G7

Sev - en - ty horns ___ of ev - 'ry shape and

C | F

kind. ___ There were cop - per bot - tom
fif - ty mount - ed

Bb | F F#dim7 C7

tym - pa - ni in horse pla - toons, ___
can - non in the bat - ter - y, ___

E | F

Thun - der - ing, thun - der - ing, all a - long the
Thun - der - ing, thun - der - ing, loud - er than be -

C7 F | Bb F

way. Dou - ble bell eu - pho - ni - ums and
fore. Clar - i - nets of ev - 'ry size and

1 C | G7

big bas - soons, ___ each bas - soon ___

— hav - ing his big fat say. There were

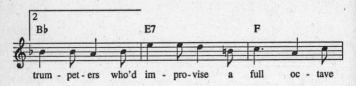

2
Bb   **E7**   **F**

trum - pet - ers who'd im - pro - vise a full oc - tave

C7   **F**

high - er than the score.   *(Instrumental)*

D7b5   **G7**

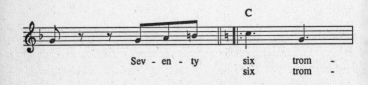

C

Sev - en - ty   six   trom -
six   trom -

Eb dim7   **G7**   **C# dim7 G7**

bones led the big pa - rade, ____ when the or - der to
bones hit the coun - ter - point, ____ while a hun - dred and

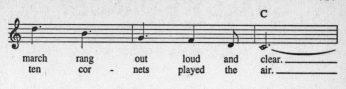

march rang out loud and clear. _____
ten cor - nets played the air. _____

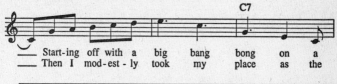

_____ Start-ing off with a big bang bong on a
_____ Then I mod-est - ly took my place as the

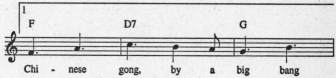

Chi - nese gong, by a big bang

bong - er at the rear. _____ Sev - en - ty

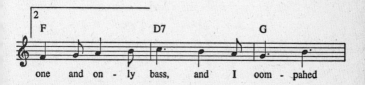

one and on - ly bass, and I oom - pahed

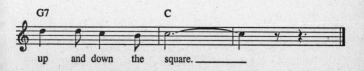

up and down the square. _____

SHALL WE DANCE?

from THE KING AND I

Lyrics by OSCAR HAMMERSTEIN II
Music by RICHARD RODGERS

Lively

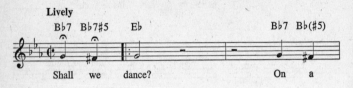

Shall we dance? On a

bright cloud of mu - sic shall we fly?

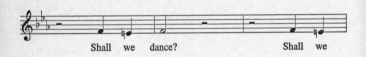

Shall we dance? Shall we

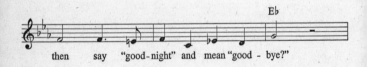

then say "good-night" and mean "good - bye?"

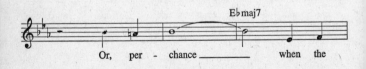

Or, per - chance _____ when the

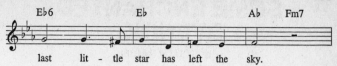

last lit – tle star has left the sky.

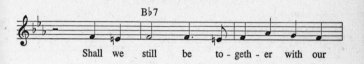

Shall we still be to – geth – er with our

arms a – round each oth – er, And shall you be my

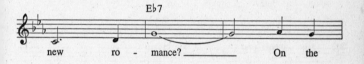

new ro – mance? _____ On the

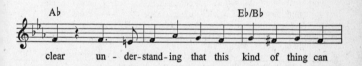

clear un – der-stand-ing that this kind of thing can

hap – pen, shall we dance? Shall we dance? Shall we

dance? Shall we dance? _____

SOME ENCHANTED EVENING

from SOUTH PACIFIC

Lyrics by OSCAR HAMMERSTEIN II
Music by RICHARD RODGERS

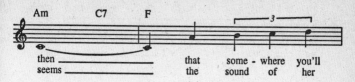

then _____ that some - where you'll
seems _____ the sound of her

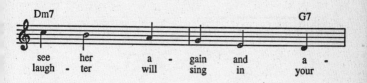

see her a - gain and a -
laugh - ter will sing in your -

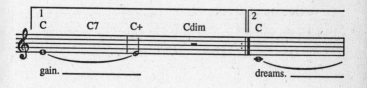

gain. _____ dreams. _____

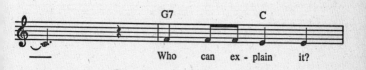

_____ Who can ex - plain it?

Who can tell you why? Fools give you rea - sons,

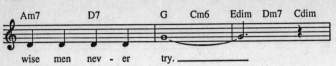

wise men nev - er try. _____

Some en - chant - ed eve - ning _____

when you find your true love, _____

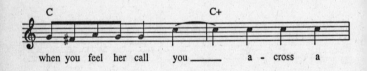

when you feel her call you _____ a - cross a

crowd - ed room. Then fly to her

side _____ and make her your

own _____ or all through your

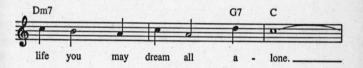

life you may dream all a - lone. _____

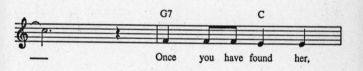

— Once you have found her,

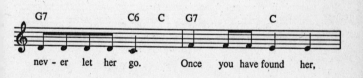

nev - er let her go. Once you have found her,

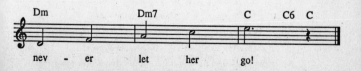

nev - er let her go!

SOMETHING WONDERFUL
from THE KING AND I
Lyrics by OSCAR HAMMERSTEIN II
Music by RICHARD RODGERS

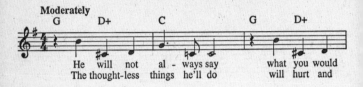

He will not al - ways say what you would
The thought-less things he'll do will hurt and

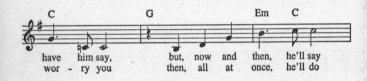

have him say, but, now and then, he'll say
wor - ry you then, all at once, he'll do

some - thing won - der - ful. some - thing

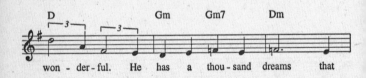

won - der - ful. He has a thou - sand dreams that

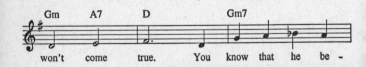

won't come true. You know that he be -

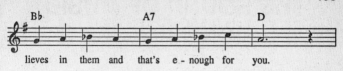

lieves in them and that's e - nough for you.

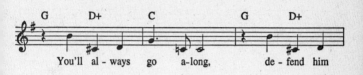

You'll al - ways go a-long, de - fend him

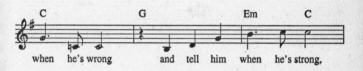

when he's wrong and tell him when he's strong,

he is won - der-ful. He'll al - ways

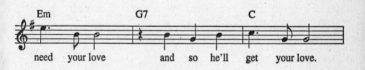

need your love and so he'll get your love.

A man who needs your love can be

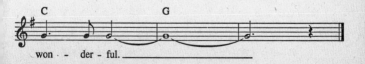

won - - der - ful. _____

THE SOUND OF MUSIC

from THE SOUND OF MUSIC

Lyrics by OSCAR HAMMERSTEIN II
Music by RICHARD RODGERS

With much expression

The hills are a - live with the sound of
go to the hills when my heart is

mu - sic. _____ With songs they have sung
lone - ly. _____ I know I will hear

for a thou - sand years. _____ The
what I've heard be - fore. _____

hills fill my heart with the sound of mu - sic. _____

My heart wants to sing ev - 'ry song it

hears. _____ My heart wants to beat like the wings of the

birds that rise from the lake to the trees. My

heart wants to sigh like a chime that flies from a

church on a breeze, to laugh like a brook when it

trips and falls o - ver stones on its way, to

sing through the night like a lark who is learn - ing to

D.S. al Coda   **CODA**

pray. I — My heart will be blessed

with the sound of mu - sic ___ and I'll

sing once more. ___

SPEAK LOW

from the Musical Production ONE TOUCH OF VENUS
Words by OGDEN NASH
Music by KURT WEILL

THE SWEETEST SOUNDS

from NO STRINGS
featured in the Wonderful World of Disney's Production
of Rodgers & Hammerstein's CINDERELLA

Lyrics and Music by
RICHARD RODGERS

The sweet - est sounds I'll ev - er

hear Are still in - side my

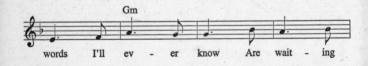

head. _____ The kind - est

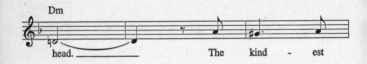

words I'll ev - er know Are wait - ing

to be said. _____ The most en -

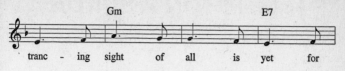

tranc - ing sight of all is yet for

me to see. _____ And the dear - est

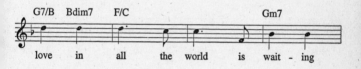

love in all the world is wait - ing

some - where __ for me, _____ is

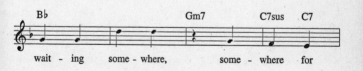

wait - ing some - where, some - where for

me. _____

TELL ME ON A SUNDAY
from SONG & DANCE
Music by ANDREW LLOYD WEBBER
Lyrics by DON BLACK

Don't write a let-ter when you want to leave.

Don't call me at 3 A. M. from a friend's a-part-ment. I'd

like to choose how I hear the news. Take me

to a park that's cov-ered with trees. _ Tell me

on a Sun-day please. Let me down eas-y,

no big song and dance. No long fac-es, no long looks,

no deep con-ver-sa- tion. _ I

204

THERE'S NO BUSINESS LIKE SHOW BUSINESS

from the Stage Production ANNIE GET YOUR GUN

Words and Music by
IRVING BERLIN

Brightly

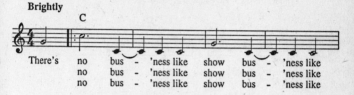

There's no bus - 'ness like show bus - 'ness like
no bus - 'ness like show bus - 'ness like
no bus - 'ness like show bus - 'ness like

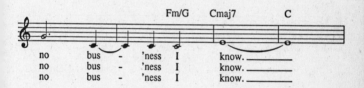

no bus - 'ness I know.
no bus - 'ness I know.
no bus - 'ness I know.

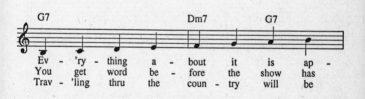

Ev - 'ry - thing a - bout it is ap -
You get word be - fore the show has
Trav - 'ling thru the coun - try will be

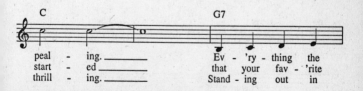

peal - ing. Ev - 'ry - thing the
start - ed that your fav - 'rite
thrill - ing. Stand - ing out in

Dm7   G7   C   Dm7/G

traf - fic will al - low. _____
un - cle died at dawn. _____
front on open - ing nights. _____

G7   Dm7   G7

No - where could you get that hap - py
Top of that your Pa and Ma have
Smil - ing as you watch the thea - tre

Am   Am7   Am7/D

feel - ing _____ when you are steal - ing _____
part - ed, _____ you're bro - ken - heart - ed _____
fill - ing, _____ and there's your bill - ing _____

D7   Dm7/G   G7

___ that ex - tra bow. _____ There's
___ but you go on. _____ There's
___ out there in lights. _____ There's

C

no peo - ple like show peo -
no peo - ple like show peo -
no peo - ple like show peo -

C7   C7/G

- ple. They smile when ___ they are
- ple. They don't run ___ out of
- ple. They smile when ___ they are

low. _____
dough. _____
low. _____

E - ven with a
An - gels come from
Yes - ter - day they

tur - key that you know will fold. ___ You
ev - 'ry - where with lots of jack. ___ And
told you you would not go far. ___ That

may be strand - ed out in the cold. __
when you lose ___ it, there's no at - tack. __
night you o - pen and there you are. __

___ Still you would - n't change it for a
___ Where could you get mon - ey that you
___ Next day on your dress - ing room they've

sack of gold. __ ⎫
don't give back. __ ⎬ Let's go on ___ with the
hung a star. __ ⎭

show. _____ There's
show. _____

TEN CENTS A DANCE

from SIMPLE SIMON

Words by LORENZ HART
Music by RICHARD RODGERS

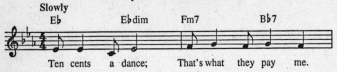

Ten cents a dance; That's what they pay me.

Gosh, how they weigh me down!

Ten cents a dance, pan-sies and rough guys,

tough guys who tear my gown!

Sev-en to mid-night, I hear drums,

loud - ly the sax - o - phone blows,

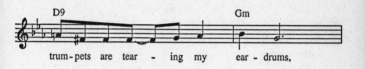

trum - pets are tear - ing my ear - drums,

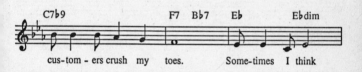

cus - tom - ers crush my toes. Some-times I think

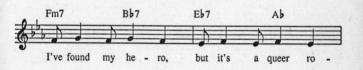

I've found my he - ro, but it's a queer ro -

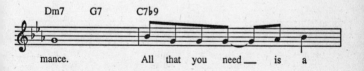

mance. All that you need __ is a

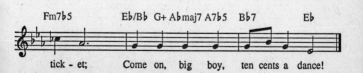

tick - et; Come on, big boy, ten cents a dance!

THEY SAY IT'S WONDERFUL

from the Stage Production ANNIE GET YOUR GUN

Words and Music by
IRVING BERLIN

THIS IS THE MOMENT

from JEKYLL & HYDE

Words by LESLIE BRICUSSE
Music by FRANK WILDHORN

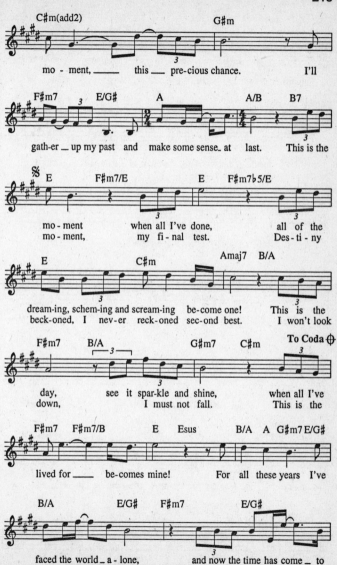

UNEXPECTED SONG
from SONG & DANCE

Music by ANDREW LLOYD WEBBER
Lyrics by DON BLACK

Gently

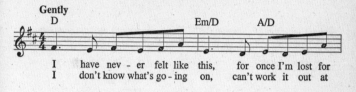

I have nev - er felt like this, for once I'm lost for
I don't know what's go - ing on, can't work it out at

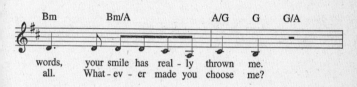

words, your smile has real - ly thrown me.
all. What - ev - er made you choose me?

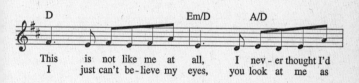

This is not like me at all, I nev - er thought I'd
I just can't be - lieve my eyes, you look at me as

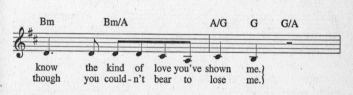

know the kind of love you've shown me.}
though you could - n't bear to lose me.}

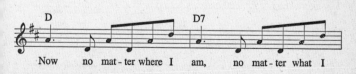

Now no mat - ter where I am, no mat - ter what I

do, I see your face ap‑pear‑ing

like an un‑ex‑pect‑ed song, an un‑ex‑pect‑ed

song that on‑ly we are hear‑ing.

hear‑ing. I have nev‑er felt like

this, for once I'm lost for words, your smile has real‑ly

thrown me. This is not like me at

all, I nev‑er thought I'd know the kind of love you've

shown me. Now no mat-ter where I

am, no mat-ter what I do, I see your face ap-

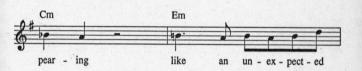

pear - ing like an un - ex - pect - ed

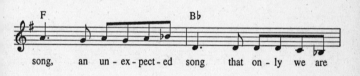

song, an un - ex - pect - ed song that on - ly we are

hear - ing. Like an un - ex - pect - ed

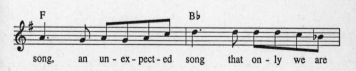

song, an un - ex - pect - ed song that on - ly we are

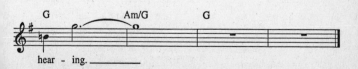

hear - ing.

THIS NEARLY WAS MINE

from SOUTH PACIFIC

Lyrics by OSCAR HAMMERSTEIN II
Music by RICHARD RODGERS

One dream in my heart, ___
One girl for my dream, ___

One love to be liv-ing for, ___
One part-ner in par-a-dise, ___

One love to be liv-ing for ___
This prom-ise of par-a-dise ___

this near-ly was mine. ___
this near-ly was mine. ___

Close to my heart she came ___

Eb	Bb	Eb
On - ly to fly a - way, _____

| Ab | Eb7 | Ab | F7 |
On - ly to fly as day flies from

| Bb | Fm7 | Bb7 |
moon - light. _____

| Eb | Fm7 | Eb/G | Eb |
Now, now I'm a - lone, _____

| Bb/D Dbdim7 | Ab/C | Abm/Cb |
Still dream - ing of par - a - dise. _____

| Eb | Cm6/A | Abmaj7 | Cm6/A |
Still say - ing that par - a - dise _____

| Eb/Bb Fm7/Bb | Eb |
Once near - ly was mine. _____

TILL THERE WAS YOU
from Meredith Willson's THE MUSIC MAN
By MEREDITH WILLSON

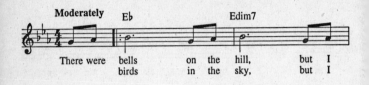

Moderately

Eb   Edim7

There were bells on the hill, but I
birds in the sky, but I

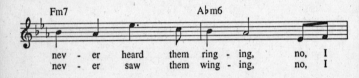

Fm7   Abm6

nev - er heard them ring - ing, no, I
nev - er saw them wing - ing, no, I

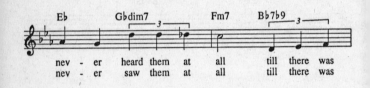

Eb   Gbdim7   3   Fm7   Bb7b9   3

nev - er heard them at all till there was
nev - er saw them at all till there was

1   Eb   Abmaj7   Bb7   2   Eb   Abmaj7

you.   There were   you.

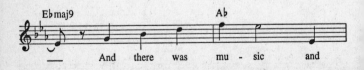

Ebmaj9   Ab

And there was mu - sic and

there were won - der - ful ros - es, they

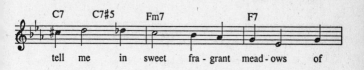

tell me in sweet fra - grant mead - ows of

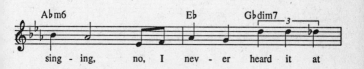

dawn, and dew. There was love all a -

round, but I nev - er heard it

sing - ing, no, I nev - er heard it at

all till there was you.

TOMORROW
from the Musical Production ANNIE

Lyric by MARTIN CHARNIN
Music by CHARLES STROUSE

Moderately slow

The sun - 'll come out _____ to - mor - row,

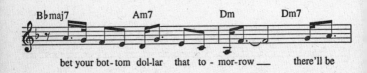

bet your bot - tom dol - lar that to - mor - row _____ there'll be

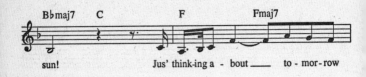

sun! Jus' think-ing a - bout _____ to - mor - row

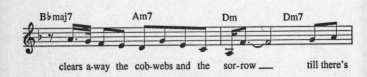

clears a-way the cob-webs and the sor-row _____ till there's

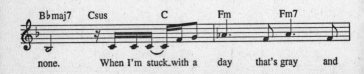

none. When I'm stuck with a day that's gray and

lone - ly, ___ I just stick out my chin and grin and

say: _____ Oh! the

sun-'ll come out ___ to-mor-row, so you got to hang on till to-

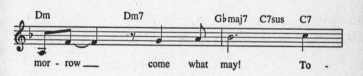

mor - row ___ come what may! To -

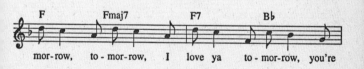

mor-row, to-mor-row, I love ya to-mor-row, you're

al - ways a day a - way! _____

TRY TO REMEMBER
from THE FANTASTICKS
Words by TOM JONES
Music by HARVEY SCHMIDT

WHAT I DID FOR LOVE

from A CHORUS LINE

Music by MARVIN HAMLISCH
Lyric by EDWARD KLEBAN

Slowly

Kiss to-day __ good-bye,
dry, __

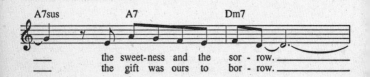

__ the sweet-ness and the sor-row.
__ the gift was ours to bor-row.

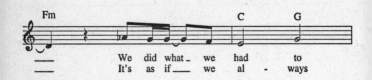

__ We did what __ we had to
__ It's as if __ we al-ways

do, __ and I can't re-gret __
knew, __ but I won't for-get __

__ What I did for love, __ What I did for __
__ What I did for love, __ What I did for __

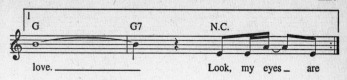

1. G   G7   N.C.

love. _____ Look, my eyes _ are

2. G   G7   G6   G   Am   Am7

love. _____ Gone, _____

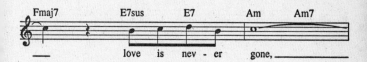

Fmaj7   E7sus   E7   Am   Am7

_ love is nev - er gone, _____

Am6   B7sus   B7   Em

_ as we trav - el on, _____

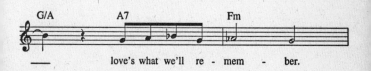

G/A   A7   Fm

_ love's what we'll re - mem - ber.

G7   N.C.   C

Kiss to - day _ good-bye _____

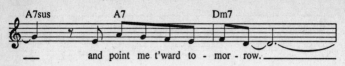

and point me t'ward to - mor - row.

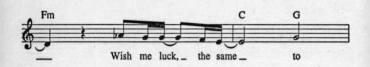

Wish me luck, _ the same _ to

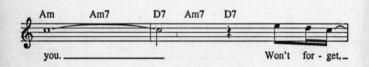

you. _____ Won't for - get, _

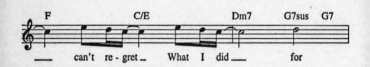

can't re - gret _ What I did _ for

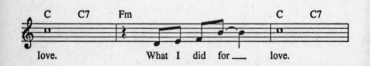

love. What I did for _ love.

What I did for _ love. _____

WITH ONE LOOK
from SUNSET BOULEVARD

Music by ANDREW LLOYD WEBBER
Lyrics by DON BLACK and CHRISTOPHER HAMPTON
with contributions by AMY POWERS

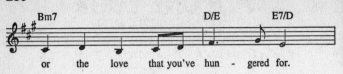

or the love that you've hun - gered for.

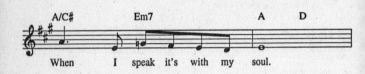

When I speak it's with my soul.

I can play an - y role. No

words can tell the sto - ries my eyes tell. Watch me

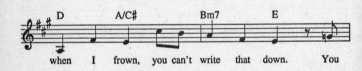

when I frown, you can't write that down. You

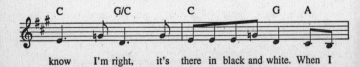

know I'm right, it's there in black and white. When I

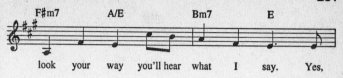

F#m7　　　　A/E　　　　　　Bm7　　　　　E

look　your　way　you'll hear　what　I　say.　Yes,

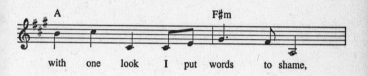

A　　　　　　　　　　　　F#m

with　one　look　I　put　words　to shame,

Bm7　　　　　　　　　　E　　　　E7/D

just　one　look　sets the　screen　a - flame.

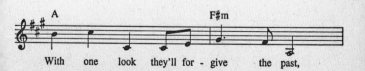

A/C#　　　Em7　　　　　　A

Si - lent mu - sic starts to　play.　　One tear

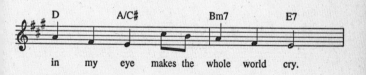

D　　　　　A/C#　　　　Bm7　　　　E7

in　my　eye　makes the　whole　world　cry.

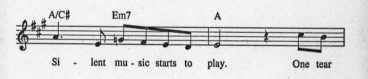

A　　　　　　　　　　　F#m

With　one　look　they'll for - give　the past,

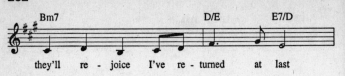

they'll re - joice I've re - turned at last

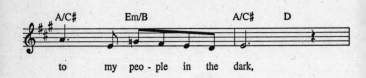

to my peo - ple in the dark,

still out there in the dark.

(Instrumental)

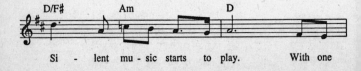

Si - lent mu - sic starts to play. With one

WHAT KIND OF FOOL AM I?

from the Musical Production
STOP THE WORLD – I WANT TO GET OFF

Words and Music by LESLIE BRICUSSE
and ANTHONY NEWLEY

Slowly

What kind of fool am I? ____ Who nev - er

fell in love. ____ It seems that I'm the on - ly

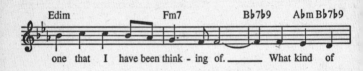

one that I have been think - ing of. ____ What kind of

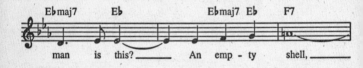

man is this? ____ An emp - ty shell, ____

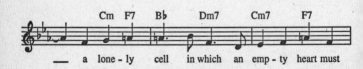

____ a lone - ly cell in which an emp - ty heart must

WHO CAN I TURN TO

(When Nobody Needs Me)

**from THE ROAR OF THE GREASEPAINT –
THE SMELL OF THE CROWD**

**Words and Music by LESLIE BRICUSSE
and ANTHONY NEWLEY**

Who can I turn to _____ when no-bod-y needs me? _____ My heart wants to know and so I must go where des-ti-ny leads me. _____ With no star to guide me, _____ and no one be-side me, _____ I'll go on my way, and af-ter the day, the

WITH A SONG IN MY HEART

from SPRING IS HERE

Words by LORENZ HART
Music by RICHARD RODGERS

Moderately slow

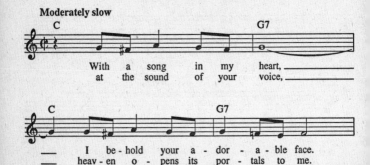

With a song in my heart, ____
at the sound of your voice, ____

____ I be-hold your a-dor-a-ble face.
____ heav-en o-pens its por-tals to me.

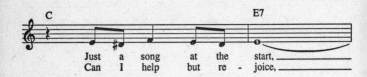

Just a song at the start, ____
Can I help but re-joice, ____

____ but it soon is a hymn to your grace.
____ that a song such as ours came to be?

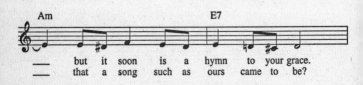

To Coda ⊕

When the mu-sic swells ____
But I al-ways knew ____

F   **Dm7**   *3*   **C6**

— I'm touch - ing your hand; _____

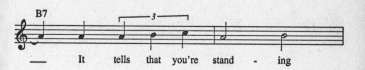

B7   *3*

— It tells that you're stand - ing

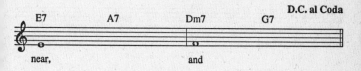

E7   **A7**   **Dm7**   **G7**   **D.C. al Coda**

near,   and

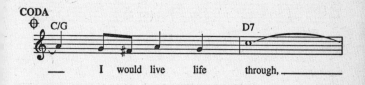

CODA

C/G   **D7**

— I would live life through, _____

C/G   **Dm7**   **G7**

— with a song in my heart for

C

you. _____

A WONDERFUL DAY LIKE TODAY

from THE ROAR OF THE GREASEPAINT –
THE SMELL OF THE CROWD

**Words and Music by LESLIE BRICUSSE
and ANTHONY NEWLEY**

On a won-der-ful day___ like to-
won-der - ful morn-ing like
take this oc - ca - sion to

day_____ I de-fy an - y cloud__
this_____ When the sun is as big
say_____ That the whole hu - man race__

__ to ap - pear in the sky.
__ as a yel - low bal - loon__
__ should go down on its knees, __

__ Dare an - y rain - drop to
__ E - ven the spar - rows are
__ Show that we're grate - ful for

plop in my eye_____ on a
sing - ing in tune_____ on a
morn - ings like these___ for the

Abmaj7   F9   **1**   F7   Fm7

won - der - ful day ___ like to - day. ___
won - der - ful morn -

Bb7   **2**   Bb7b9   Eb   Fm7

___ On a - ing like this. ___

F#dim7   G7   Ab

___ On a morn - ing like this ___

Ab+   Ab6

___ I could kiss ev - 'ry -

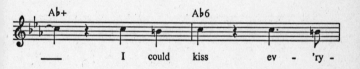

Ab7   Adim7   Eb   Fm7   Bb9

bod - y I'm so full of love ___ and good -

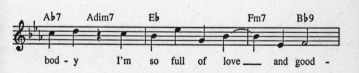

Ebmaj9   Eb6   Eb7   Ab

will. ___ Let me say fur - ther - more ___

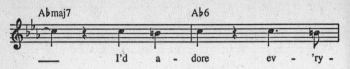

I'd a - dore ev - 'ry -

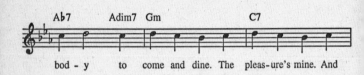

bod - y to come and dine. The pleas-ure's mine. And

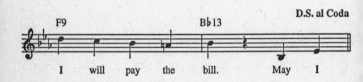

D.S. al Coda

I will pay the bill. May I

CODA

world's in a won - der - ful

way, _____ on a won - der - ful day __

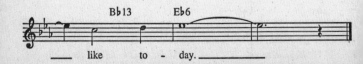

__ like to - day. _____

A WONDERFUL GUY

from SOUTH PACIFIC

Lyrics by OSCAR HAMMERSTEIN II
Music by RICHARD RODGERS

Moderately bright

I'm as corn - y as Kan - sas in
I am in a con - ven - tion - al

Au - gust, I'm as nor - mal as
dith - er, With a con - ven - tion - al

blue - ber - ry pie. No more a
star in me eye. And you will

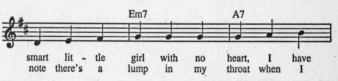

smart lit - tle girl with no heart, I have
note there's a lump in my throat when I

found me a won - der - ful guy! ___
speak of that won - der - ful

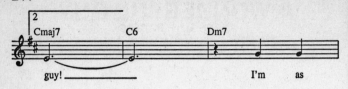

guy! _____ I'm as

trite and as gay as a dai - sy in

May, A cli - ché com - ing true! _____

I'm bro - mid - ic and bright as a

moon hap - py night Pour - ing light on the

dew! _____ I'm as corn - y as

Kan - sas in Au - gust, High as a

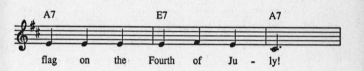

flag on the Fourth of Ju - ly!

If you'll ex - cuse an ex - pres - sion I

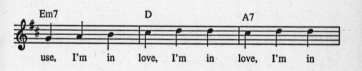

use, I'm in love, I'm in love, I'm in

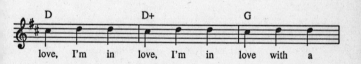

love, I'm in love, I'm in love with a

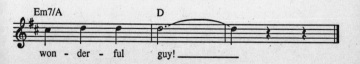

won - der - ful guy! _____

YOU TOOK ADVANTAGE
OF ME
from PRESENT ARMS

Words by LORENZ HART
Music by RICHARD RODGERS

Moderately

Ebmaj7 · Edim7 · Fm7 · Bb7
I'm a sen-ti-men-tal sap, that's all. ___

Gm7 · F#dim7 · Fm7 · Bb7
What's the use of try-ing not to fall? ___ I

Bbm7 · Eb7 · Abmaj7 · Db7
have no will, ___ you've made your kill ___ 'cause you

Gm7 C7 Fm7 · Bb7 Ebmaj7 Fm7 · Bb7 Ebmaj7 · Edim7
took ad-van-tage of me! I'm just like an ap-ple

Fm7 · Bb7 · Gm7 · F#dim7
on a bough, _____ and you're gon-na shake me

Fm7 · Bb7 · Bbm7 · Eb7
down some-how, ___ so what's the use? ___ You've

Abmaj7 · Db7 · Gm7 C7 Fm7 · Bb7
cooked my goose ___ 'cause you took ad-van-tage of

YOU'LL NEVER WALK ALONE
from CAROUSEL

Lyrics by OSCAR HAMMERSTEIN II
Music by RICHARD RODGERS

Moderately

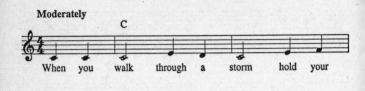

When you walk through a storm hold your

head up high and don't be a-

fraid of the dark. ___ At the

end of the storm is a gold - en

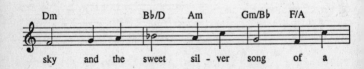

sky and the sweet sil - ver song of a

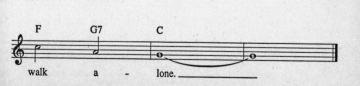

YOUNGER THAN SPRINGTIME
from SOUTH PACIFIC

Lyrics by OSCAR HAMMERSTEIN II
Music by RICHARD RODGERS

Moderately

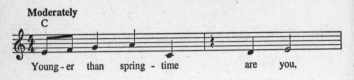

Young-er than spring-time are you,

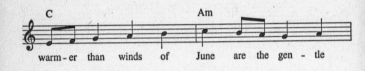

soft-er than star-light are you,

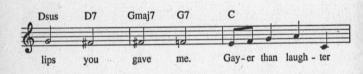

warm-er than winds of June are the gen-tle

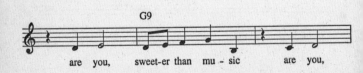

lips you gave me. Gay-er than laugh-ter

are you, sweet-er than mu-sic are you,

GUITAR CHORD FRAMES

	C	Cm	C+	C6	Cm6

C

C#	C#m	C#+	C#6	C#m6

C#/Db

D	Dm	D+	D6	Dm6

D

Eb	Ebm	Eb+	Eb6	Ebm6

Eb/D#

E	Em	E+	E6	Em6

E

F	Fm	F+	F6	Fm6

F

This guitar chord reference includes 120 commonly used chords. For a more complete guide to guitar chords, see "THE PAPERBACK CHORD BOOK" (HL00702009).

	C7	Cmaj7	Cm7	C7sus	Cdim7
C					
C♯/D♭	C♯7	C♯maj7	C♯m7	C♯7sus	C♯dim7
D	D7	Dmaj7	Dm7	D7sus	Ddim7
E♭/D♯	E♭7	E♭maj7	E♭m7	E♭7sus	E♭dim7
E	E7	Emaj7	Em7	E7sus	Edim7
F	F7	Fmaj7	Fm7	F7sus	Fdim7

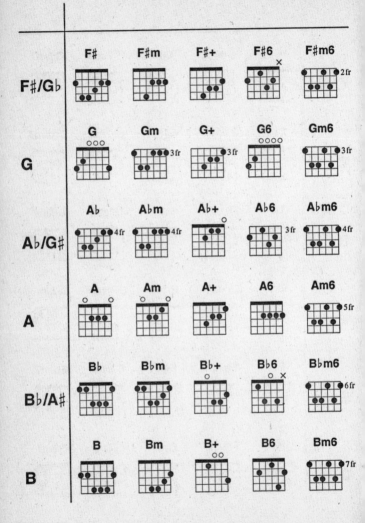

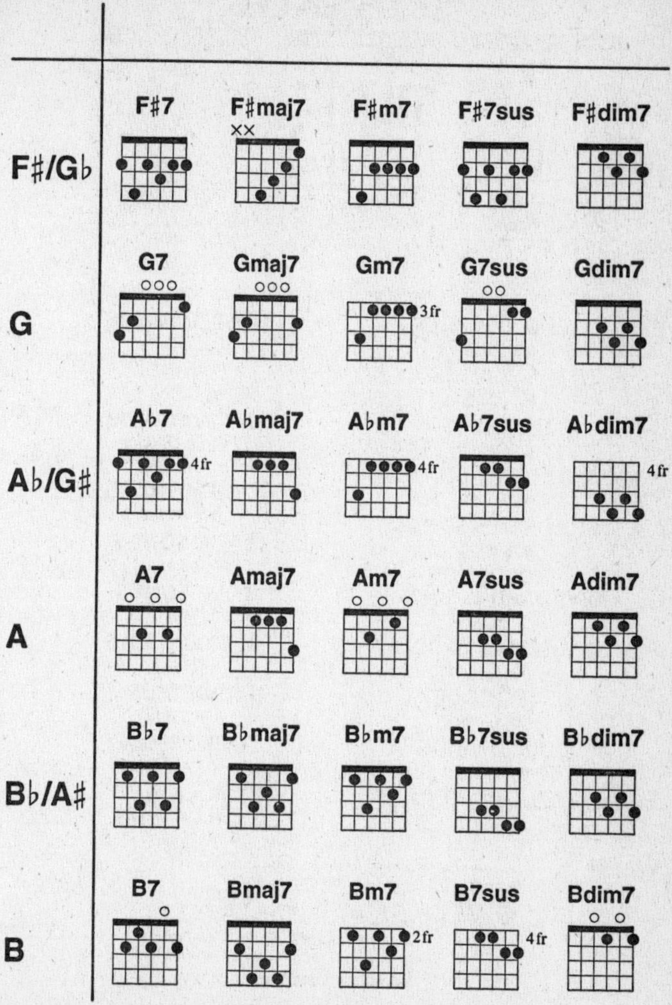
F♯/G♭
F♯7
F♯maj7
F♯m7
F♯7sus
F♯dim7
G
G7
Gmaj7
Gm7
3fr
G7sus
Gdim7
A♭/G♯
A♭7
4fr
A♭maj7
A♭m7
4fr
A♭7sus
A♭dim7
4fr
A
A7
Amaj7
Am7
A7sus
Adim7
B♭/A♯
B♭7
B♭maj7
B♭m7
B♭7sus
B♭dim7
B
B7
Bmaj7
Bm7
2fr
B7sus
4fr
Bdim7